'Highly readable while being challenging and pragmatic. Applying the advice in this excellent book will improve your strategic effectiveness.'

Paul Walsh, CEO, Diageo – the world's leading premium drinks company

'In a fast moving, globalizing world, Chris shows us practical ways to develop robust strategies and, more particularly, to implement them.'

Nadir Godrej, Managing Director, Godrej Industries – one of India's most diversified conglomerates

'In *Making Strategy Work*, Chris Outram distils decades of experience, advice and perspective on how to execute a good strategy into an easy-to-read handbook that will benefit any executive looking to take their business to the next level. The book takes effective, complex theories and breaks down how and why they work, making it an invaluable primer on what is new in corporate strategic development.'

John Brock, Chairman, Coca Cola Enterprises – one of the world's largest Coca Cola bottlers

'A joy to read something about strategy that is down to earth and gives the protagonist's perspective. Packed with practical tips for bosses at every level, including ideas I haven't seen anywhere else.'

Richard Koch – a leading author of best selling business books

Making your strategy work

Making your strategy work

How to go from paper to people

Chris Outram

PEARSON

Harlow, England • London • New York • Boston • San Francisco • Toronto • Sydney • Auckland • Singapore • Hong Kong
Tokyo • Seoul • Taipei • New Delhi • Cape Town • São Paulo • Mexico City • Madrid • Amsterdam • Munich • Paris • Milan

PEARSON EDUCATION LIMITED
EDINBURGH GATE
HARLOW CM20 2JE
UNITED KINGDOM
TEL: +44 (0)1279 623623
WEB: WWW.PEARSON.COM/UK

First edition published 2013 (print and electronic)

ISBN: 978-1-292-00259-0 (print)
978-1-292-00285-9 (PDF)
978-1-292-00284-2 (ePub)
978-1-292-00778-6 (eText)

British Library Cataloguing-in-Publication Data
A catalogue record for the print edition is available from the British Library

Library of Congress Cataloging-in-Publication Data
Outram, Chris.
Making your strategy work : how to go from paper to people / Chris Outram. pages cm
Includes bibliographical references and index.
ISBN 978-1-292-00259-0 (pbk.) -- ISBN (invalid) 978-1-292-00285-9 (PDF) --
ISBN (invalid) 978-1-292-00284-2 (ePub) -- ISBN (invalid) 978-1-292-00778-6 (eText)
1. Strategic planning . 2. Organizational change--Management. I. Title.
HD30.28.O885 2013
658.4'012--dc33
2013022715

10 9 8 7 6 5 4 3 2 1
17 16 15 14 13

Cover design by Two Associates

Print edition typeset in 11pt Myriad Pro by 3
Print by Ashford Colour Press Ltd., Gosport

NOTE THAT ANY PAGE CROSS REFERENCES REFER TO THE PRINT EDITION

Contents

About the author

Chris Outram has been a strategy consultant for more than 30 years. In that time he has consulted to a multitude of corporations around the world in many industry sectors. In 1987 he co-founded OC&C Strategy Consultants, which has grown to be a major challenger to the more established, usually US-founded firms and now boasts more than 450 consultants, operating out of nine countries around the globe. OC&C conducts strategy assignments designed to enhance their client's commercial success in a value creating and sustainable way. Prior to his career in Strategy Consulting, Chris honed his managerial skills with firms such as The Mobil Oil Co and Air Products. Chris graduated from Birmingham University with a Double First in Mechanical Engineering and Industrial Economics and was awarded an MBA with Distinction from INSEAD.

Preface

The idea of writing a book about strategy as part of the celebrations to mark OC&C's 25th birthday in 2012 was one that I immediately rejected once it became clear to me that I would be the one who would be burdened with this rather daunting task.

After a few weeks' thought, however, I reconsidered on two conditions. The first one related to the pragmatic observation that our clients (Chief Executive Officers, divisional managers, etc.) are intensely time poor and do not want to (and probably would not even attempt to) read through 500 pages of OC&C's musings on the subject of strategy. Secondly, even though I passionately believe that OC&C is one of the best strategy consultancies in the world, our observations about strategy are likely to be only part of the answer.

In addition to the views of our 68 partners, therefore, I suggested we talk to more than 100 of the world's leading executives about what happens in reality and how they think about and implement strategy – and then encapsulate this in a very short book.

So what we have done is to create a guide to what matters to senior executives when thinking about and executing strategy. Yes, the views of OC&C's partners and associate partners are incorporated in the text, but so too are the views of people like Bob McDonald, the former CEO of Procter & Gamble, as well as Zhang Ruimin, the former CEO of the Haier Group, the world's biggest white goods company. (Short biographies of the 100-plus interviewees and contributors can be found at the end of the book. And their photographs are reproduced, with their kind permission, inside the front and back covers.)

As a result, the book now reflects both the theory and the practice of strategy development with a preponderance of the latter.

The reader will find the essentials of good strategy development in addition to many hints as to what can go wrong (and how to avoid it) when implementing strategy.

You will read about the 'Conspiracy Theory of Management' as well as the 'Ripple Theory of Engagement'. Neither are truly theories – they are more about how things work in the real world but because we are consultants at the end of the day we could not resist the word 'theory'!

We believe that this book is unique in focusing on what to do to implement good strategy rather than just developing it.

We hope that you agree with me, OC&C's 68 partners and the more than 100 CEOs who have contributed.

* * *

A book like this does not get written without a huge number of contributions. If anything, *Making Your Strategy Work* is a rather extreme example of a large number of contributions and a relatively small number of pages. I cannot remember who wrote it but whoever said that it is more difficult to write a short note than a long one was definitely prescient.

It is difficult to know where to start to acknowledge those who have contributed but the original idea for a book came from one of my OC&C partner colleagues, David Sinclair.

I will forgive him eventually!

The other partners of our firm also made excellent contributions, whether via the very constructive inputs of our editorial committee, comprised of Pieter Witteveen, Michel Sasportes, Bjoern Reineke, Nic Farhi and Serge Blanchard (note the polyglot nature of this team); the great support of our International Managing Partner, Chehab Wahby; or the countless memos and emails I received, along with a detailed survey of all of OC&C's Partners and Associate Partners.

Our firm thrives on this type of collaboration, whether it is on projects like this book, assignment teams or joint teams with our clients. Without this collaborative gene OC&C would not be the outstanding firm it is today.

Thanks also has to go to those at OC&C who helped create other elements of the content, such as researching all academic and commercial contributions on the subject of strategy (Laura Taylor), creating case studies and analysing survey data (Anthony Gent, Amanda Crawford, Alon Zadka and Christoph Treiber) or allowing me to plagiarize their ideas (James George, who originally developed the 'Six (now Ten) Deadly Sins of Strategy'). Thanks also to Cinthia Chen for her help in China. I would also like to thank Alon Zadka of OC&C for his substantial contribution to the creation of Chapter 8.

Inside OC&C, thanks must also go to my long-suffering assistant, Jo Falcon, who has scheduled more interviews than either of us care to remember and has typed up my recollections thereof faithfully.

But even more important has been the contribution of Danika Gill who has managed this project from start to finish. She is rightly a hard taskmaster and the fact that this book is being printed broadly on time and in good shape is entirely down to her and her relentless pursuit of a great outcome. Thank you, Danika.

We have both been helped by the editorial and publishing skills of Peter Kirwan, Tess Read, Annabel Wright and John Bond of whitefox, who have been tireless in their pursuit of a quality product.

External to OC&C, I must recognize the contribution of Richard Koch, himself a prolific writer of such tomes as *The 80/20 Principle* and *Superconnect*, who not only generously offered lots of excellent insight and guidance but even went so far as to allow me to retreat to his beautiful hacienda in Spain to gain the peace and quiet to write this book.

But the biggest thanks of all must go to the 100-plus executives who donated their time to talk with us about strategy and to share their experiences, both good and bad. Their perspectives have been instrumental in shaping our thoughts about what is really important as opposed to what is merely interesting. I will not pick out any contributions in particular, even though some produced amazingly insightful perspectives on what really works and what does not, and how to mobilize the major resource pool of any company – its people.

I have been privileged that this book's creation has given me the opportunity to be the conduit through which all these inputs have found their way on to the page.

Chris Outram
Co-Founding Partner, OC&C

Foreword

When Chris Outram told me he was invading my book-writing territory, I didn't expect it to be like this. To be honest, I anticipated a thick treatise with all kinds of elaborate strategies – after all, OC&C are very focused and only 'do' strategy, and they are probably the only serious firm that can still make that claim.

I was therefore rather relieved to read the book you have in your hands.

How much more is there to say about strategy? Not much, in my opinion. The great merit of this book is that it follows a different tack.

Chris asks how do you 'make' strategy and make it work in practice. OC&C's answer is that, if a firm has a halfway decent strategy or better, success lies in the execution of the strategy. And very little intelligent stuff has been written on that. Why? Because most academics and consultants consider execution a tedious detail.

This book explodes that myth. Instead, it says, execution is nine-tenths of the gap between bliss and bankruptcy. If the road to hell can be paved with sophisticated strategies, the only people worth listening to are those who know from experience which road leads up to the clouds, and which gravitates to the nether regions. Strategy signage won't tell you. Only CEOs can. So, at some large cost in time – the only thing a consultant will recognize as both precious and finite – Chris and his partners went to talk to more than 100 CEOs from around the world.

The CEOs they met are all successful, yet at some stages in their careers they have all been scarred by brushes with the low road. They know what works and what doesn't because they've been there. And they say some surprising things.

Have you heard of the Conspiracy Theory of Management? I hadn't. But it's one of the best ideas I've ever encountered. Once you've read it, I bet you'll say, 'Of course!' and do things differently. And the same can be said of the Ripple Theory of Engagement.

So I won't detain you any more – crack on and read this now. You have nothing to lose but your delusions; you have a wonderful world to win.

Richard Koch
Author of *The 80/20 Principle* and *The Financial Times Guide to Strategy*

Introduction

'The only worthwhile strategy is one which can be executed.' JUSTIN KING, CEO, J. SAINSBURY

The panic that set in when I first sat down with a blank screen to write this book was palpable. With 25 years of OC&C behind us, surely our 68 partners had something to say about strategy. And yet the more I thought about it, the greater my panic. What ultimately broke the logjam and led to the words that follow was the realization that strategy is not just about the conceptual wrestling we do helping our clients solve some of the most intractable problems in the world. More importantly it is what you do with the strategic advice. How do you make the strategy work?

And that's when the cumulative experience of our 100-plus CEO interviewees and OC&C's 68 partners started to make sense. Thinking about strategy has to be intimately linked with what can be done with it. And what is that linkage?

People ... starting from the CEO downwards.

But let us start at the beginning – strategy development (rather than execution) – and ask ourselves, given that strategy as a discipline has been around for 50 years or so, 'What's new in corporate strategy development?'

In trying to answer this question, I can almost hear the groan from the reader. If there's one thing the world doesn't need, I hear you mutter, it's another book about strategy.

As Claus-Dietrich Lahrs, the CEO of Hugo Boss AG, puts it: 'By now, the number of books about strategy probably exceeds the number of viable and sensible strategies developed in the history of capitalism.' He's right, of course. So why have we written another one?

After all, the commonly accepted definition of strategy is more or less the same as it was 50 or so years ago. That is not to say it is always correctly understood. Dr Fritz Oesterle, former CEO of Celesio, notes: 'Strategy is one of the most misused terms today; too often, everything that companies cannot explain properly is labelled "strategy" or "strategic".' In essence, however, strategy is all about defining a differentiated – and value-creating – direction for your company. It focuses attention, mandates the allocation of resources and delivers the objectives of stakeholders (usually some combination of shareholder value, customer satisfaction and/or employee engagement).

'Remember whose career is on the line.'

Designing strategy requires brainpower, as well as a selection of tools and techniques. Yet neither of these requirements has changed very much during the past 25 years.

What has changed is the context in which we develop strategy. Globalization, the internet, technology, regulation, the sheer pace of change and the need to demonstrate sustainability: all of these factors have become major contenders for the attention of any leadership team thinking about strategy.

As a result, management's role in strategy development has changed. Senior executives must be more intimately involved with strategy development, particularly the CEO. The process they pursue may be more inclusive. But in an increasingly complex world, full of short-term pressures, the buck continues to stop at the CEO's desk. As Stephen Page, the former Chief Financial Officer

(CFO) of United Technologies Corporation, told us: 'Consensus is always good. But remember whose career is on the line.'

Stuart Fletcher, CEO of Bupa, believes that CEOs should focus on four things: strategy, people, reputation and performance – in that order. 'And when I say strategy,' he adds, 'I don't mean the design of it, but the doing of it.'

Fletcher rightly emphasizes the risks of execution. Implementation is where the rubber hits the road. 'When things go wrong, it's usually because strategy hasn't been implemented properly,' says Sir Terry Leahy, Tesco's former CEO.

Why does this happen? How can we stop it? That's what this book is (mostly) about: avoiding the bad things that often occur when a good strategy is put into action and what we can learn from the greats who successfully implemented a winning strategy. We offer some guidance about what middle and senior management can do to further the company's strategic health.

The senior management team's role in strategy execution has not changed fundamentally. But the potential consequences of action and inaction have changed.

Unless the leadership is willing to make increasingly tough – often people-related – calls, there's a good chance that even the most robustly designed and planned strategy will fail.

In order to help business leaders grapple with these issues, we have identified ten pitfalls waiting to engulf the unprepared. Additionally, we will make some suggestions (as all good consultants should do) in the subsequent chapter about how to avoid them.

Finally we will boil all of this down into some advice for incoming business leaders. We'll look at how he or she should start the perilous journey to the Strategic Promised Land – a place of long-term value creation and enduring and rewarding employment (plus, of course, a modicum of enjoyment and reward for the boss).

Traditionally, books need to have an author's name on the spine. This one is no exception: my thoughts on strategy comprise a large part of what you're about to read. But we're a firm that believes in collaboration. Accordingly, I have leaned heavily on two sources of insight. The first is a group of CEOs: our customers and potential customers. In a marathon effort over several months, we have interviewed more than 100, and you'll find their thoughts on strategy all the way through the book.

Our 68 Partners and 23 Associate Partners are my second source of insight. In July 2012, we surveyed all of them, asking them to comment on 13 hypotheses about strategy development and implementation. You'll find their views in these pages, too.

This book has been written for those who are in the early stages of their careers as CEOs, managers and business leaders, as well as for those who are more experienced. What follows is the distillation of 25 years of experience of *Making Your Strategy Work*.

Developing good strategy – a science or an art?

'If everyone likes the strategy, it is probably wrong!' ANDY GREEN, FORMER CEO, LOGICA (NOW CGI)

When the management writer Richard Koch was preparing the fourth edition of *The FT Guide to Strategy*,[1] he asked ten leading strategists for their assessment of important developments in the field during the previous 10–15 years. There had been plenty of developments. In fact, the ten experts came back with what Koch calls a 'staggering 30 new insights or methodologies'. But there was a catch: none of the experts really agreed with each other about which of these developments were important. In fact, only four of the 30 insights or methodologies were cited by more than one of the experts. The lack of consensus was telling.

If you're cynical, you might conclude that slick marketing – the ability to dress up the same old ideas in a variety of fancy new outfits – is the most important skill a strategy guru can hope to possess. No doubt there's some truth in this.

When I first told my strategy consulting colleagues that I thought we were in an industry with limited product or process innovation, I thought that I might be in danger of being lynched as a heretic. But then our CEO interviewees saved the day. For they clearly saw that even though developing strategy is relatively straightforward, it is not easy. And let's also give the academics and strategy professionals some credit: they have offered up new perspectives. Around the edges, strategists have also refined techniques designed to stimulate strategic thinking. For example, academics at the business school INSEAD have developed the Blue Ocean approach to thinking about markets – that is, putting open water between yourself and the next competitor[2] (see Chapter 4, 'Why the top team must lead the charge').

Despite this, some companies appear to have forgotten what strategy is about. For them the planning process begins with high-level assumptions about GNP or inflation, before progressing to high-level goals such as a demand for 10% profit growth, or maximized cash flows. Managers therefore think about cost-cutting, avoiding expensive confrontations with competitors, or cancelling investments designed to gain market share.

The result is an incremental vision that typically supplies modest growth in the context of good (but never surprising) financials. To break the logjam, at OC&C we use a technique called End-Gaming, which invites management to define where they want to be before worrying about how to get there.[3] This is a technique whose principles inform the forward-thinking decisions IMI CEO Martin Lamb makes about the shape of his company: 'You need to populate your company with people who can cope with whatever complexities there will be in five years' time, not just today.'

Both the End-Gaming and Blue Ocean strategy approaches encourage management to move beyond a short-term focus and to think instead about where the 'Strategic Promised Land' might be. How you get there is also very important, but is dealt with as a secondary issue. Having bold goals and failing to reach them is usually better than having mediocre ones and achieving them.

Strategy development has moved on in another way, too: we now have access to much more data about the businesses we run, and the markets in which they operate, than we did two or three decades ago. Our ability to process that data is much enhanced.

'More data + less time = poor decisions'

But the fundamental insights into what matters – and why – have not changed. The way in which we analyse markets, customers, suppliers and competitors largely remains the same. In his book, Koch describes these traditional methods as 'old verities'. Some of them date back not to the 1950s, but the 1850s. Indeed in Babette Bensoussan and Craig Fleisher's 2008 book *Analysis without Paralysis*, they identified '10 Tools to Make Better Strategic Decisions'.[4] All ten had been designed in the previous century!

If there really is very little that is truly new, then what's so special about strategy development? Shouldn't we all be able to do it in our sleep? Not quite. Unfortunately, a lot of what passes for strategy is often insufficiently rigorous and objective. There are at least five reasons why this happens inside organizations:

1 **Lack of attention to detail:** this often results in the collection of inadequate (or irrelevant) data, some or all of which is processed inappropriately. As Jez Maiden, CFO of National Express, puts it: 'More data + less time = poor decisions.'
2 **A false sense of security:** it's easy to ignore fundamental shifts in the structure of an industry, to lull yourself into accepting business as usual.
3 **Underestimation:** companies frequently underestimate what the competition (particularly the left-field competition) might be able to achieve.
4 **Overestimation:** companies very often overestimate the power of their own business model, their own staff.
5 **Over-elaboration:** most strategies can be boiled down to the need to get a few things right. If you overcomplicate your strategy, then you risk people not understanding it, including those who most need to come to grips with it: the employees. 'Strategy has to be simple,' insists former

> CFAO Management Board Chairman Richard Bielle. 'It shouldn't be a book that only experts can read. If it is complex, it means it is unfinished.'

All of these failings are avoidable, and the best way of avoiding them is for the leadership team to take charge of the strategy process, lending it validity, insight and teeth. Accept no substitute for this kind of involvement. Above all, don't delegate strategy development. You may choose to work with an in-house strategy professional or an outside consulting firm, but, as CEO, it is you who remains fully accountable. 'The CEO has to be the Chief Strategy Officer,' says Sir Terry Leahy, former CEO of Tesco. 'This cannot be abdicated, as it's ultimately the CEO's and the board's responsibility.'

The board also needs to play a role in supporting and communicating strategy. In our view, this is an area where plenty of room for improvement exists. It's telling that our interviewees were very vocal on this score. 'Communication is the most undervalued tool in business,' says Justin King, J. Sainsbury's CEO. 'You can never communicate too much.'

Penny Hughes, a serial Non-Executive Director, insists that boards 'need to embrace and not receive strategy'. She goes on to criticize boardroom discussions of strategy where 'management delivers a finished plan up to the board, and the board receives it without engaging with it too much'. Instead, Hughes argues, boards should insist that managers explain themselves, their ideas and the available options. 'Management needs to clarify why it prefers one option to all of the others,' she says. 'Without a proper cross-examination, the board cannot be fully committed to management's strategy.'

'Ask the question: "If we fail, why will we have failed?"'

Sir Nigel Rudd, Chairman of BAA and Invensys, agrees: 'The non-executives need to be involved in the formulation of strategy and the review of the options. They should not just listen to management's choice of their preferred option.'

Charles Sinclair, Chairman of Associated British Foods, takes the argument further. 'Best practice requires you to take the board on the same strategic journey as the CEO,' he says, 'The non-executives need to understand the choices and how they were prioritized. They should also know what keeps the CEO awake at night. In addition, why not have the "pre-mortem" now? Ask the question: "If we fail, why will we have failed?"'

The process of strategy development itself should always rely upon a rigorous review of eight things:

1. **Customer needs:** who needs what and why? How much might they be willing to pay for it?
2. **Market trends:** what is changing and why? Do we understand where these changes will take the market (and us)?
3. **The competition:** what are our competitors – the obvious and not-so-obvious ones – doing and why? Do we understand their strategies? Can we find ways to outpace them?
4. **The economics of participating:** how can we make money in a sustainable way? How much will this cost? Do we understand the economics of our (potential) models and those of our actual and possible competitors?
5. **Positioning and capabilities:** how are we different? Is our level of differentiation sufficient to sustain our strategy? Can we resource our efforts with the right people, working in the right roles?

6. **Radical option elaboration:** without taking risks, rewards are often meagre. Are we taking on enough risk? Have we been as bold as possible?
7. **Financial modelling:** in describing our strategy financially, does it all fit together? Can we afford it? Will it satisfy our stakeholders?
8. **Looking ahead to execution:** are we clear about what we need to achieve? Do we understand what needs to be done and who will be accountable for specific parts of the plan? Have we got the right people to execute the strategy? What are the milestones for tracking success? What are the potential mitigating factors if some of the bets we make prove unsuccessful?

None of this is rocket science. But as with all processes, there are a few nuances. For example, how do you ensure that the strategy development remains vibrant, exciting and creative? How do you avoid 'personal and corporate staleness'? As Patrick Coveney, CEO of food wholesale giant Greencore, puts it, 'You have to make sure you build constructive discontinuities into your strategy process.'

If the process becomes moribund or discredited, you may as well shut down the entire effort. Little or nothing comes out of processes that have been devalued in this way.

'Do not undertake the strategy process just because it is in the calendar,' says Ian Livingston, CEO of BT Group. 'Do it because there is something not right with the current strategy, or because you think you can improve it.' It's unwise to repeat the same strategy development process every year. The process can become stultifying, especially if it starts to become a kind of 'pre-budget' arena for political manoeuvring.

The results of this can be disastrous. In research we conducted for this book internally at OC&C, one of our partners pointed to companies where this happens. 'Strategy should be about taking a fundamental look at positioning and market dynamics,' this partner noted. 'But when it becomes part of the political process that surrounds budget-setting, incremental thinking starts to dominate everything. In this context, managers have a strong incentive not to overpromise, to avoid radical steps. This completely destroys the strategic process.'[5]

John Goodwin, the CFO of The LEGO Group, draws a sharp distinction between strategy and budgeting. 'Performance/operational improvement is not a strategy. It is more to do with budgeting,' he says. 'Strategy should focus on the deep pools of profit that can sustain a company in the long term.' For most companies, a 'drains up' process every two or three years should suffice with a light-touch update in the intervening year(s) to deal with changing circumstances. Online and technology businesses with short half-lives are an exception to the rule. As one of our partners notes: 'For most industries, three years might be too frequent. But in the case of something like the mobile phone industry, three years is far too long an interval. Using that time frame, you would end up sleepwalking through the rise of Apple and the demise of Nokia.'

Charlie Mayfield, Chairman of John Lewis, uses this approach: 'We don't review our core strategy each year, but instead assess where we need to change course or emphasis, always within the context of how we see the market developing in the future.'

Market pressures can also affect the frequency with which strategy needs to be revised. Jean-François Palus, Deputy CEO of PPR, notes, 'Twenty years ago, you could establish a three- to five-year strategic vision, share it with the financial markets and they would take it. But nowadays you are required to explain what you're doing and why you're doing it every three to six months.' As Constantino de Oliveira Jr, Chairman of GOL, the leading Brazilian airline, says: 'Strategy needs to be dynamic as competitors can usually mimic a successful strategy and thus you need to move to the next series of strategic moves rapidly.'

Another way of keeping the process alive, of ensuring that it gets prosecuted enthusiastically, is for the CEO and the leadership team to show real commitment. The CEO's attitude, in particular, acts as a bellwether for the rest of the organization. If he/she gives the strategy process a lot of credibility then so will everyone else. Ideally, the CEO must display a preference for strategy based upon:

- Penetrating insights rather than simple descriptions of markets.
- Challenge and boldness rather than business as usual.
- Competitive differentiation rather than performance benchmarking.[6]
- Ideas that are simple and communicable, rather than complex and unfocused.
- Plans that are doable rather than fantastical.
- Approaches that are engaging and purposeful, rather than anaemic and inhuman.

As Barry Judge, CMO of Living Social, says: 'Generally, companies underestimate what is required in a good strategy process, starving it of resource and ending up with an inadequate answer.' David Feffer, Chairman of Suzano, puts it this way: 'Strategy is important and the process of thinking about strategy is an important way of thinking fundamentally about your business in a structured manner.' But as long as you remember these prerequisites and have access to talented and experienced practitioners of strategy development, then it should be possible to arrive at a strategy that is differentiated and which creates value. Anything less is inexcusable.

* * *

In summary, in some ways, very little has changed in strategy, other than new tools for developing it, such as the End-Gaming and Blue Ocean methods, which encourage management to move beyond a short-term focus and to think instead about where the 'Strategic Promised Land' might be. But in another way, strategy development has changed dramatically – we now have access to much more data about the businesses we run, and the markets in which they operate, than we did two or three decades ago, and our ability to process that data is much enhanced. This means that while the analytical tools for strategy development remain the same, the process of analysis is much more complex. There are many reasons why strategy development inside a company may fail to provide a useful outcome, and so to give the process the best chance of success it is vital that the CEO take charge of the strategy process, giving it validity, insight and teeth.

A strategy review must encompass seven areas of questions beginning with the customers' needs:

- Who needs what and why?
- What are the market trends: where will any changes take the market?
- Who are our competitors? Do we understand their strategies, and can we outpace them?
- What are the economics of participating? Do we understand the economics of our (potential) models and those of our competitors?
- How are we different, in terms of positioning and

capabilities? Are we different enough and do we have sufficient resources to sustain our strategy?

- Does our financial strategy add up to profits that will satisfy shareholders?
- Are we clear about what we need to achieve and how to achieve it?

In leading the strategy process, the leadership should be aiming to achieve penetrating insights rather than simple market description, challenge and boldness rather than business as usual, competitive differentiation rather than performance benchmarking, simple and communicable ideas and doable plans with approaches that are engaging and purposeful.

What makes strategy development difficult nowadays?

'Change is the only constant.' PHILIPPE HOUZÉ, CHAIRMAN OF THE EXECUTIVE BOARD, GALERIES LAFAYETTE

The process of strategy development may be straightforward but that does not make it easy. The context has changed fundamentally in the last decade. As a result, the role of the CEO has changed, too. Our cohort of CEOs consistently underlined this point.

'The assumption that you are in control of events is wrong and dangerous. Adaptiveness is a key component of strategy,' says Sir John Sunderland, former Chairman of Cadbury Schweppes and currently a Non-Executive Director of Barclays Bank. 'Strategy is a route map to a destination. Unfortunately the maps you use are necessarily a little fuzzy. There are lots of uncharted volcanoes and chasms ahead of you.'

Between them, the 100-plus CEOs we interviewed identified seven core reasons why it has become more difficult to develop strategy:

1 Globalization

This factor has been a feature of strategy development for a long time. More recently, and, somewhat accelerated by the arrival of recession in the developed world, the challenges posed by globalization have changed subtly. In the era of Globalization 1.0, which started with the fall of the Berlin Wall and the opening up of the Chinese economy in the 1990s, companies in the developed world mostly regarded the BRICs (Brazil, Russia, India and China) as relatively unsophisticated export markets.[1]

Globalization 2.0 is a more complex phenomenon. Today, emerging economies are developing all of the hallmarks of sophisticated consumerism. By 2040, the Organisation for Economic Co-operation and Development expects that more than 50% of the goods and services sold to the world's middle classes will be purchased in China and India.[2] Companies need to be fully integrated into these economies in order to compete effectively.

Globalization 3.0 promises to be even scarier. Fuelled by domestically generated revenues, Chinese companies are starting to compete in earnest in the West's core markets. They have the time to get it right, the ambitious people to make it happen and the requisite access to financial markets. The recent landmark deal whereby the state-owned Chinese company Bright Food acquired a majority stake in Weetabix, the iconic British cereal brand, hints at what's on the horizon.

'The assumption that you are in control of events is wrong and dangerous.'

Bob McDonald, former CEO of Procter & Gamble, warns of an end to any lingering complacency. 'The BRICs are now markets in their own right requiring tailored products, local brands and customized routes to market. They will be competing with us in our traditional markets in the next decade.' Paul Walsh, the CEO of Diageo, agrees. 'Countries like Brazil are no longer a nice little earner,' he says, 'they're now core to our future. Soon enough, we will see Indian whiskies and Brazilian cachaça becoming part of the competitive set in our traditional markets, in the same way that Russian vodka has.'

Not only are the BRICs changing in size and significance, their direction of travel is changing, too. As Jim Muehlbauer, former

CFO of Best Buy, puts it: 'Historically many of the BRIC countries had economies that were relatively small and moving in the same direction. Today, those markets are huge. And their growth rates are fluctuating and diverging.'

As if that were not enough, what about the impact of globalization on the implementation of strategy?

As Claus-Dietrich Lahrs, the CEO of Hugo Boss, observes: 'Globalization increases the need to execute well. We have to communicate where our company is heading; why it is worthwhile (and fun) to work for us; and we need to tell employees – in many different languages, across hundreds of cultures – why we value their contribution.'

We are truly in the era of Globalization 2.0.

2 Technology

The speed of technological change continues to accelerate. This is hardly new, but it's increasingly important, and we're not just talking about the impact of the internet, either. The key differentiating factor continues to be your company's ability to tune into the technosphere to identify emerging technologies and then rapidly exploit (or defend against) new trends. 'The real challenge,' says Iwan Williams, former Managing Director, Grocery and Bakery of Premier Foods, 'is to get managers to embrace, not just understand, the digital arena.'

Accelerating technological change creates a need to anticipate complex scenarios and identify decisive moves at previously unknown levels of complexity. Just ask the TV manufacturers that have made a rapid transition from plasma to LCD to LED screens.

They'll treat you to a compelling discourse on what happens when high-velocity technological change combines with huge capital expenditure costs in a market full of fast followers. Consumers want to buy the resulting products, but it is extremely hard for producers to turn a profit. Sony, for example, lost an average of $45 on every television set it sold during 2011.[3]

Thierry de la Tour d'Artaise, Chairman and CEO of SEB, has watched the market change. 'The product cycle keeps getting shorter,' he says. 'We are in the business of selling electrical appliances, and we're now introducing the concept of a collection that sits on retailers' shelves for only six months, just like fast fashion in the apparel business.' Nancy McKinstry, CEO of Wolters Kluwer, notes that 'disruptive technologies used to come around once a decade, now they seem to be annual events'. As Rick Hamada, CEO of Avnet, Inc., says: 'The increasing rate of change is relentless – the wonderful world of technology is never the same any two days in a row.'

Michel Combes, the former CEO of Vodafone Europe, cites the iPhone as an example of the speed with which things can change. Apple entered the mobile handset market with the launch of the first generation iPhone in mid-2007. Five years on, Apple has sold around 260 million iPhones worldwide, generating cumulative revenues of $150bn. Samsung's volumes may be bigger, but Apple lays claim to the majority of profits generated by the sector.[4] 'A few, short years ago Apple was not even on the radar in terms of mobile phones,' says Combes. 'Today, they probably have more customers in Europe than Vodafone.'

Gavin Darby describes the velocity of technological change in the communications industry as 'frightening'. 'The winners are Google, Apple, Facebook and Amazon,' he says. 'The identity of the losers – Nokia, Motorola, RIM and possibly Microsoft – is surprising, given that they were (and mostly remain) huge concerns. It's extraordinary to observe the speed at which companies can grow, peak and then slide. This is a lesson to us all in corporate humility.'

3 The internet

The internet remains the most disruptive influence on strategy in the 21st century. It continues to have a profound impact in three ways: the increasing availability of data; the multifaceted rise of networking; and the continuing explosion of business models that trail in its wake.

Data availability

We have access to vastly greater volumes of data than a decade ago, and the expansion of potential data sources will not stop any time soon. 'There's so much of it!' says Lawrie Philpott, former head of Coopers & Lybrand's UK HR Practice and founder of Philpott Black. 'It's like drinking water from a hosepipe. But we still need to support our strategies with it. Remember: in God we trust. From everyone else, I want data.'

Some would argue that we are already overloaded with more sources of information than we can handle. The endless stream of data can be exhausting, says Doug Ivester, former Chairman and CEO of The Coca-Cola Company. 'It used to be a real problem for us. We found that the sheer volume of data we needed to gather and present was leading to fatigue, rather than insight and enthusiasm.'

'In God we trust. From everyone else, I want data.'

All of this puts a premium on our ability to turn data into information and, ultimately, into knowledge. Ron Sandler, former

Chairman of Northern Rock, bemoans the problem: 'The ability to access, process and display information has destroyed people's appetite for strategic thinking, and has left companies feeling jaded.' Getting hold of the right data in a timely way, processing it so that it becomes informative and then extracting actionable knowledge from it: this ability has been vastly amplified as a core skill in modern strategy development.

Digital business models throw off vast amounts of data. The success of companies such as Amazon and Google is based largely on the way they have crunched, studied and exploited information about their users. Now, the culture of continuous analysis is becoming more broadly entrenched. 'Data-driven businesses test new propositions and marketing strategies on a daily basis against control groups,' says one of OC&C's partners. 'These companies are using data instead of hypothesizing about the world around them.'[5]

Bob McDonald, former CEO of Procter & Gamble, sees evidence of progress. 'We are trying to turn information into a competitive advantage,' he says. 'We are "democratizing" it by getting it to the desktop where its instant availability will reduce hierarchy and politics.'

But – and there is always a but – some have also made the point that information is never the whole answer.

Data-mining can become mechanistic. 'The data doesn't always indicate latent demand,' says one of our partners. 'Sometimes, looking for white space can lead to a better strategy.' In addition, the ability to synthesize remains as important as it ever was. 'Strategy is about understanding the detail of your business,' says another of our partners. 'But it's also about not getting lost in the detail. The challenge is to distil the decisive insights from data. Then you have to connect these insights within a bigger picture.'[6]

Sjoerd Vollebregt, CEO of Stork, the Dutch holding company, argues that in the context of information overload, managers 'should not underestimate the value of common sense, experience and intelligent judgement'. Luiz de Mendonça, CEO and President of Odebrecht Agroindustrial agrees: 'With so much data around accessible to all, the key issue is "What on earth is the most important insight that can be obtained from it?"'

Networking

Networks have always mattered, but the internet has increased their importance. Inside organizations, they can be used – formally and informally – to share knowledge. Externally, loose networks of customers can be used to feed back insights about products and services. On a personal level, platforms such as Facebook, LinkedIn and Twitter allow us to leverage our own personal networks. All of these applications have one thing in common: they're powered by the internet. The internet allows human beings to take advantage of their basic underlying social instincts in an entirely new and unique way.

Sensibly, the management writer Richard Koch extols the virtues of having wide, but often relatively weak, personal networks of contacts (precisely the kind of networking enabled by social platforms). 'If I do not know something,' says Koch, 'I may know someone who knows someone who does.'[7] At the age of 57, Paul Walsh, CEO of Diageo, will never qualify as a digital native. But that doesn't let him off the hook. 'It is almost impossible to imagine a world without the internet and instant consumer feedback,' he says. 'It is not my generation, but I have an internet expert come in every couple of weeks to show me what is out there.'

This might sound odd – even absurd – to digital natives reading this book. But for individuals as well as companies, there's no escape – at least not if you want to compete with everyone else on a level playing field. And when I say 'everyone else', I mean it. One recent study asked 1,400 college students in the developed world what they would do if they were offered a job with a company that banned access to social media in the workplace. Well over half – 56% – said they would either reject the job offer, or accept it and then try to find a way to circumvent corporate policy. Separately, two-thirds of respondents said they planned to ask about social media policy at forthcoming job interviews. That's how important social networking is for the talent of tomorrow.[8]

New business models

Since the late 1990s, the internet has enabled countless innovative business models. Many have gone mainstream. The internet long ago started to dominate what we might call its heartland markets: any business in which there is a need for information, news and research, easy ordering, simple payment and/or customer tracking. But the internet's work is not done. Its disruptive potential continues to expand. The arrival of high capacity broadband networks, for example, means that the word 'broadcasting' may soon become obsolete. (In the UK, television signals recently switched from analogue to digital; soon enough, 'broadcasters' may abandon the airwaves altogether, reaching us instead via broadband networks.) This is only one example: in medicine, the car industry and manufacturing, the arrival of cheap and plentiful bandwidth promises to bring with it a new generation of disruptive business models.

If you want to know what the future looks like, take a look at the media industry, where the internet has been wreaking havoc for the past 15 years. 'In the media industry, there are now the traditional players and the internet-based creative destroyers,' says Bernd Kundrun, former CEO of Gruner + Jahr and now a board member at RTL, one of Germany's leading TV channels. 'These approaches are totally at odds. I think about the contrast in terms of airspace. In one of these worlds, we have jumbo jets flying at 10,000m altitude, carefully separated by air traffic controllers. The other approach involves a swarm of small, but highly manoeuvrable aircraft, all trying to get off the ground, all trying to gain altitude. Other industries will soon start to experience something similar. Retail and mail order are not far behind the media industry.' As Luiz de Mendonça, CEO and President at Odebrecht Agroindustrial, puts it: 'The environment has become intensely complex. It's like two-dimensional chess has suddenly become three-dimensional.'

The message here is to work out whether your business is likely to be threatened. If the answer is yes, be willing to cannibalize yourself rather than letting others do it. Move early or you may find that you will not be able to move at all. And do not worry (too much) if the business declines somewhat in the process. A smaller business is better than no business at all. Nor is it uncommon for digital businesses to generate better margins than their old analogue equivalents (especially if the latter are in steep decline).

As if all this were not enough, then there is the overlay of mobility.

Current predictions say that we will be doing a lot of what we historically did on our home computers on our mobile devices – smartphones, tablets or PCs. This opens even more avenues up for rapid information flows, networking and new business models. There are few industries that can afford to be complacent in the light of this avalanche of consumer-oriented technological innovation.

4 Pace

Today, information moves around the world at quicksilver speed. When errors occur, corporate and personal reputations can be made or destroyed within seconds. Communications have, therefore, become a critical element of strategy – and its implementation. Communications to employees, customers and investors can make or break a strategy.

The speed with which information is transmitted has always mattered. In 1815, Nathan Meyer Rothschild received news of Wellington's victory at Waterloo before anyone else in London. At the time, British government bond prices were depressed by the prospects of a Napoleonic victory. Putting his knowledge to work, Rothschild scooped up vast quantities of British government bonds at bargain prices and made a killing.

Today, everybody is a Rothschild, with access to breaking news services on desktop screens and mobile handsets. It's widely accepted that markets function with maximum efficiency if investors all have simultaneous access to validated information. This is the basis of a vast regulatory effort designed to inhibit insider trading in financial markets.

In the real world, however, access to information often remains asymmetrical. Strategists can use this to their advantage. For example, when one of the three players in Britain's liquid milk industry announced that it would be the first to build a billion litre processing plant, rivals were immediately forced to shelve their own plans for similar mega-dairies. The industry could not absorb that much capacity. A simple announcement sealed the fate of the other two competitors.

Parm Sandhu, former CEO of Unitymedia, notes that 'a clear strategy gives people a framework for action and tactics'. All three are certainly intimately related. And in some industries (media and online retail in particular), tactics and strategy are melding. 'Stractics'™ is the much-discussed new priority. Stefan von Holtzbrinck, CEO of Holtzbrinck, the German family-owned media company that is globally invested in education and book publishing businesses, believes that 'in the digital-only world, decision timescales are collapsing and our strategy processes need to adapt to that speed'.

'In the digital-only world, decision timescales are collapsing.'

For Charles Sinclair, Chairman of Associated British Foods, strategy and tactics are 'increasingly a continuum – a dynamic and continuous duo'. Something similar has happened at Vodafone, where former European CEO Michel Combes says strategy development has been transformed. 'A decade ago, we would do a plan for the next three to five years, and we would update it every three years,' says Combes. 'This approach is now impossible. Today, we run an inclusive strategy exercise every year, and then we adjust it on the fly with messages from the executive committee. You could say that we have moved to planning at management board level on a monthly basis.'

Even an annual cycle is not sufficient for some. One of our partners at OC&C takes a more fundamentalist view: 'In a fast-moving environment, annual process sets a rigid frame. People think strategy for two months a year and then forget about it. Strategy should be a daily concern, a mindset, not a yearly exercise.'[9]

The internet demands flexibility. Strategy has to be developed rapidly and, if necessary, adjusted rapidly. 'Be careful of the illusion of certainty which emanates from having a three-year plan,' says Stuart Fletcher, CEO of Bupa. 'Be vigilant! You need to have long-term vision and goals but do not allow them to shut your eyes and ears about what is happening around you.'

Yet despite the fetishization of speed, it isn't always an essential component of success. Microsoft wasn't a first-mover in the market for desktop operating systems. Neither was Apple the first company to manufacture tablets and touch screens. 'They understood it was about more than speed,' says one of our partners. 'There's a need to define the product or experience successfully, and that's what they did.'[10] Among some of our partners, there is also a suspicion that speed-to-market is declining in importance, precisely because digital technology erases barriers to entry. Speed might well help, but it's equally important to design a better mousetrap than your competitors.

'Sometimes you need to change the route to avoid hitting a recently erected brick wall.'

The timescales for large investments haven't necessarily changed, either. An oil refinery is still an oil refinery: it will operate for 25 years or more. That's the time frame you'll need to consider when making an investment of this kind. Closer to home, IT/systems investments last five to ten years. These, too, need the backing of a good long-term strategy.

So for many companies, strategy does need to stretch beyond the short to medium term. You need to imagine the geopolitical and technological factors that might affect the value of the investment. Can these risks be discounted? Are they at least justifiable? Very often, this requires a profound understanding of the here and now, as well as the near-term future.

'Strategy is a journey,' says John Goodwin, CFO of The LEGO Group. 'Sometimes you need to change the route to avoid hitting a recently erected brick wall.'

5 Regulation, compliance and values

Navigating your way around regulation has become harder and harder. Whether it's food standards, health and safety, financial regulation or carbon emissions, much needs to be understood and complied with.

Of course, regulation has always existed. It has always been manipulated, too: in Europe before the Second World War 'non-tariff' barriers to trade were prevalent including government support for particular industries, quotas and licensing requirements that made it difficult for foreign competitors to conform to local needs. Nevertheless, tariff barriers came down, and free trade expanded across the globe, the world's population became more affluent. The inevitable result has been generalized pressure for higher ethical and safety standards. Indeed, technology has occasionally created risks so large that they naturally call forth regulatory oversight (as in the case of nuclear power generation, for example). The pace of change leaves governments and international bodies struggling to keep up with necessary regulatory changes.

But what about corporate values? Here we are not just talking about compliance with regulation, but compliance with something more intangible: the standards and behaviours that the public expects from companies that trade with, and

'A culture of excellence and decency will eventually win out.'

against, each other. In short, we're talking about what most people would describe as ethics.

One has to be pragmatic.

Inevitably, compliance with norms that operate in the developed world isn't universal. In some cases, the behaviour of companies in nations that have only recently become full participants in world commerce lags behind what is expected of their competitors in the developed world. In the context of developing strategy, this can present a problem. 'Governance in Europe can be burdensome compared with what a Chinese company has to endure,' says Luke Jensen, Group Development Director at J. Sainsbury.

On the other hand, as Bob McDonald, former CEO of Procter & Gamble, points out, authenticity is important. 'You just do not have a choice,' he says. 'Put your values on a pedestal and live and celebrate them. A culture of excellence and decency will eventually win out. Our aim is to make sure that values are an integral part of our business model. If they are (and they are), we will prevail.'

Nevertheless, defence and aerospace businesses in the developed world inevitably find themselves doing business with counterparties who just do not have the same legal and ethical standards. This tension remains in place. The only antidote is compelling product. This puts the seller in a commanding position to set the rules.

6 People

Human capital is so important that we're going to devote an entire chapter to it later on. For now, let's just note one point, which was echoed by many of our interviewees: the shortage of talented and experienced executives continues to be a constraint. And the more the world's economy grows, the greater the shortage becomes. Doug Ivester, former Chairman and CEO of The Coca-Cola Company, sees this very much as the CEO's remit: 'The CEO should be his or her own HR person – it's his or her responsibility to make sure the right people are in place. Once they are, your execs can then function as their own talent managers.'

'People deployment is a critical part of our strategic arsenal,' says Paul Walsh, CEO of Diageo. 'We have to keep reviewing and developing our top executives. We compare their current and future roles against the strategic market matrix to make sure that we have the right people in the right place. My only advice here is to make sure that you are wary, that you are not assessing people through rose-tinted glasses. Getting this right is fundamental to the strategy.'

In an increasingly globalized world, attracting and retaining talent is becoming an increasingly difficult task as opportunities arise and are publicized on a global basis. StepStone's Global Talent Barometer survey is finding increases year on year in the percentage of people globally who wish to work abroad. The 2012 survey found that only 14% of the surveyed workforce did not wish to work abroad.

7 Sustainability and purpose

Increasingly, the great firms in the world are adding sustainability and purpose to the strategic agenda. It's their belief that these issues will become important differentiators, and eventually a *sine qua non* for participation in most markets. This is our belief, too. In the long run, we believe that these factors will become even more important than mere compliance with regulations. This is largely because your ability to gain access to the best employees can make or break a strategy.

And nowadays when employees choose to work for one company instead of another, being able to demonstrate sustainability and that it has a corporate purpose are often factors in the decision-making process. Accordingly, demonstrating sustainability, personality and purpose will become an important part of most companies' internal communications.

'Volatility is now a given in most businesses.'

Harsh Mariwala, the founder, Chairman and Managing Director of India's Marico, agrees. 'Sustainability is important to recruits,' he says. 'They care about these things and if we ignore them, we do so at our peril.' No longer is strategy just about making money (although that is still important for the capital markets). It's also about a company's broader purpose and their constructive participation in society – and, in turn, what these say about the individuals who work there. Benet Slay, CEO of Carlsberg UK, emphasizes the distinction between the two goals: 'Make sure you understand your purpose, not just that of the business.' This kind of purpose can be a differentiating factor.

'Volatility is now a given in most businesses, certainly ours, and it is a strength that our purpose does not change,' says Bob McDonald, former CEO of Procter & Gamble. 'On the other hand, our strategy might need to change from time to time to deal with that volatility.' A sense of purpose can go a long way to differentiating your company. Tim Steiner, CEO of Ocado, the fast-growing web-based grocery business located in the UK, has built this assumption into his business model. Even though many of Ocado's employees are pickers and lorry drivers, Steiner insists that they all need to 'feel proud of what they are doing and that they are an integral part of your strategy'.

Andy Prozes, former CEO of LexisNexis and currently in private equity, agrees. 'People want to feel that they are successful at what they do, but they also want to feel they're doing more than making money for shareholders.'

* * *

Globalization, technology, the internet, regulation, the war for talent, pace, sustainability and purpose: all of these factors have complicated the process of strategy development. None of this represents a major or sudden shift. In fact, all of these trends represent progression along a continuum of change that started some decades ago. It's also true that the complications I've outlined in this chapter have become much more relevant to some businesses than others. Long term, however, this shift towards ever-greater complexity will affect all sectors of the global economy.

As Sir George Buckley, former CEO of 3M, says: 'You have to work hard at strategy – you do not just walk down a Namibian beach expecting to find diamonds in the sand!'

The way in which leadership teams balance these complex and sometimes conflicting forces has become a critical part of strategy development.

In summary, we live in a constantly changing world. Our lives are ever more disrupted by radical evolutions in technology and transformational innovations in business models. The increasing pace of change is a relentless challenge and the accompanying changes in regulations and laws, as governments and regulators everywhere try to keep up with the revolutions around them, provide further shifting environments which every business has to adapt to in order to survive, let alone grow. It is vital that CEOs take decisions to invest strongly in people, make commitments to develop sustainably, and foster a sense of purpose in their company's growth to compete effectively in this ever more globalized world.

Why the top team must lead the charge

'Don't just talk about it: do it!' DR ROLF KUNISCH, BOARD MEMBER AND FORMER CEO, BEIERSDORF

The much-maligned and much-discussed topic of leadership is critical in the increasingly complex world of strategy development. 'You have to develop leaders,' says Bob McDonald, former CEO of Procter & Gamble. 'Deciding strategy is relatively straightforward. Getting it to work is not. That's where leadership comes in.'

Once upon a time, the world was relatively simple and predictable. A CEO could rely on a Director of Strategy to deliver the company's strategy. Indeed, the head strategist probably came from a consulting company, and, therefore, could bring best practice to the party.

Unfortunately, this is no longer enough.

The role of the CEO in the strategy process has become increasingly critical. 'However participative the process, there is no doubt that strategy is still the rightful purview of the CEO,' contends Luke Jensen, Group Development Director at J. Sainsbury. In a world where the amount of available data is growing exponentially, yet insight remains in short supply, the CEO and the top team must lead the strategy process, intervening to provide guidance and direction. 'It takes a strong CEO to create the time and the process, as well as the atmosphere required to develop good strategy,' advises Cees 't Hart, CEO of FrieslandCampina, the Netherlands' leading dairy company.

There are seven key areas in which the contribution of the CEO, in collaboration with the senior management team, will be decisive:

1 Design: involving the right people

The team that is responsible to the CEO for helping to get strategy over the line is key and needs to be chosen carefully. 'The responsibility for the execution of strategy is tightly held among no more than 10–20 people and within that the CEO's leadership is fundamental to its success,' says Penny Hughes, a Non-Executive Director of RBS.

On this score, Luke Jensen has some advice: 'In the leadership team supporting the CEO, you need a combination of brainy, sometimes non-linear thinkers and "doers", who know how things work. If you are a CEO who is not very strategic, then make sure that you have someone on your team who is. And make sure it's someone whose advice you value.' Jim Muehlbauer, former CFO of Best Buy, agrees. 'The lack of talent to design strategy is an issue,' he says. 'Strategy is dealing with fundamental and complex questions like "why do we exist?", "what is our purpose?" and "what are we here to do for people?" You need special people to answer these non-obvious, but critical, questions.'

In terms of generating the strategy itself, most agree that it is vital that the process invites participation from many levels in the company. 'Involve a lot of people early,' says Rainer Hillebrand, Vice-CEO of Otto, Germany's leading mail-order company. 'It makes it easier in the later implementation stages.'

On the other hand do not overdo it. 'I need 52,000 people involved in implementing our strategy,' observes Stuart Fletcher, CEO of Bupa. 'But I do not need 52,000 people involved in developing it.'

You can secure participation in a variety of ways: through consultation, workshops, surveys and subcontracting some of the key modules to internal task forces.

At the lower levels in a company's hierarchy, you needn't give employees access to the full picture. (They probably won't have the training and contextual knowledge to make sense of it.) But your employees do have a massively important contribution to make: they will be critical to the implementation of the strategy eventually. They are more likely to implement it well if they feel that they have been part of its creation and understand their role within it. As Cláudio Bérgamo dos Santos, CEO of Hyper Marcas, says: 'We focus on making sure that employees buy into our purpose and become part owners and feel that they can act entrepreneurially. Just being an employee is not enough.' Roberto Prisco Paraiso Ramos, Chairman of Brazil's Odebrecht Oil and Gas, agrees: 'Strategic action plans need to cascade down the organization, creating high levels of accountability and entrepreneurship.'

2 Scope: framing the question(s)

Again, this sounds simple. But it's not. Often, the strategic question you really need to ask is less obvious than it seems. For example: we often get asked to design strategies for entering the Chinese market. In many cases, the real question that needs answering is whether or not the company in question should be in China in the first place. The difference is important.

Being clear about the question that you, as a member of the leadership team, are asking will help to produce a clear answer. Here's a particularly good (if open-ended) one, posed by Harsh Mariwala, founder of Marico, India's rapidly growing fast moving consumer goods (FMCG) insurgent: 'What is our right to win and how will we do it?'

3 Guidance: providing a hypothesis

In the consulting industry, it has long been recognized that a deductive approach to strategy development just doesn't work in our information-saturated world. Boiling a massive ocean of available data in order to deduce the answer is impractical.

Instead, inductive reasoning is a far more efficient approach to strategy development. Here, the process begins with an informed hypothesis, which the consulting team sets about either proving or disproving.

In the same way that insight differs from information, a hypothesis differs from a scenario. A hypothesis is a structured view of the potential answer. A scenario is mere description: it describes a set of conditions, a context, and implies that you may need a distinct strategy to address these conditions best. Strategy is always set within a scenario.

Interestingly, it does not much matter whether you:

- prove the original hypothesis is right,
- prove that with a few amendments it is right, or
- disprove it, but home in on an alternative hypothesis which really will work.

In a relatively efficient fashion, any one of these three routes will lead you to a viable strategy.

Clearly, it's important that the inductive approach doesn't become an excuse for the senior management to propose a pet theory, the essential wisdom of which is confirmed by yes men and yes women. The process needs to open up sufficient space for debate. This is the only guarantee that good analysis will prevail.

Andy Green, former CEO of Logica, agrees: 'Accept robust and personal challenges – it will make you better strategically.'

Applying the right degree of constructive challenge in the process will ensure that the probability of gaining true and differentiated insight is maximized. Unfortunately, this requires time and that is one commodity that business leaders have little of.

Objectivity and challenge are essential elements of any good strategy process. Rob van den Bergh of NV Deli Universal, concurs. 'The process of strategy has not really changed – and it is often improved by bringing a few gifted outsiders to the table to provide discipline and rigour.'

4 Quality control: ensuring that the right data is processed rigorously and creatively

Covering the right ground sounds easy enough: market analysis, customer needs, competitor review. It's a straightforward list. But the problem is that many companies fall into the trap of describing these things rather than analysing them. Andy Harrison, CEO of Whitbread, describes himself as 'a great believer in analysis – it allows one to make smaller leaps of faith'.

There's a difference between information and insight. 'You can often find some data somewhere to support your argument,' cautions Dalton Philips, CEO of Morrisons. 'The CEO has to be central to the thinking so that he or she can judge what is really joined up versus what is not.'

Description alone is of little or no use. What the executive team needs is perspective, which explains how markets work and why competitors behave in the way that they do. This takes rigour, rather than the business-as-usual mindset that's so common in many companies. In order to get this, the senior management need to set out what they require, or to get help setting out what they require (either from in-house strategy experts or from a trusted consulting partner).

On this question, partners at OC&C have a variety of views. 'There are companies out there that are pretty good at challenging themselves,' says one. Another contributor to our internal survey goes further: 'Some of the most successful businesses we've seen in the past five years – Amazon, Google, Tesco – have invested heavily in building out their own strategy teams. In the right organization, equipped with the right resources, the results can be genuinely impressive.'[1]

If you're going to build up internal resources in this way, do it properly. There's no point in an internal strategy unit that fails to cut the mustard because it lacks a powerful voice within the organization, or the resources to deal with the large number of incoming projects. Our partners have encountered teams of this kind, too.

Winning strategies do not grow on trees. You will have to work really hard to identify how you can compete and win. If you have not done this before, you may not have a good sense of the detailed way in which the analysis has to be performed in order for it to be useful. The information you work with must amount to more than a description of markets, customers and competitors. It needs to yield insight. At every stage of the process, the requirement must be: insight, insight, insight. Nothing less will do!

On the other hand there are alternate ways of getting this objectivity and challenge. The company's board often has a wealth of senior and experienced executives who could offer such challenge.

5 Boldness: making sure that the team has been sufficiently radical

There is no downside to considering bold and potentially risky moves. 'Strategy should consider the bold and the ambitious,' says Claus-Dietrich Lahrs, CEO of Hugo Boss. 'It should raise questions, provoke and even cast doubt on things. This creates the curiosity to explore different strategic options.'

Tim Steiner, CEO of Ocado, is no stranger to risk. 'Nowadays strategy needs to be bold,' he says. 'In many industries, winner does take all. Google is a good example. When Google launched Gmail, it was a late entrant into the market for web mail. So it offered users several hundred times more storage capacity than any competing system. By the time everyone else had caught up and storage costs had collapsed, it was too late. Google had established a viable foothold in the market.'

'Strategy needs to be bold.'

You need to ask questions such as:

> 'Have we thought about how to defend against challengers?'
>
> 'Have we considered making our own company into a challenger and acting as a challenger might do?'
>
> 'If we were the majority shareholders, what would we do?'

Many strategy processes suffer from assuming that the status quo will remain broadly constant in the future. In these times of rapid and sometimes unpredictable change this is a very dangerous assumption to make and one that has crippled many companies and some industries. However you choose to do it, you need to have a challenging process to tackle these assumptions. The alternative isn't worth contemplating. Living with a 'Motherhood and Apple Pie' view of strategy which lulls the organization into a false sense of security should not be tolerated (see Chapter 7, 'Ten strategic pitfalls ...'). The stakeholders will be badly served and the longevity of the CEO and senior management dramatically reduced.

'It's quite hard to be too bold,' says Gavin Darby, former CEO of Cable & Wireless Worldwide, and currently CEO of Premier Foods. 'The alternative, incrementalism, is a route to a slow death because someone is going to outrun you.' The US airline industry suffered from this attitudinal problem when the low-cost carriers led by Southwest Airlines entered the market. The traditional airlines did little to change their business models, hampered by ingrained business processes, an innate lack of boldness and a recalcitrant labour force. Little wonder that the low-cost airlines now account for about 45% of the market value of US airline companies.

There is really little excuse for this 'head in the sand' approach to strategy. There are many ways in which this type of 'futurology' can be introduced into the strategy process:

- Invite experts from outside the company to talk to the strategy team.
- Use consultants on 'what is the future shape of the industry'.
- Design the process to include the analysis of challenger strategies (and the economics thereof).
- Use techniques such as End-Gaming and Blue Ocean to raise the sights of the strategy team to 'unreasonable' levels.
- Set 'unreasonable' strategic goals.

The last two approaches are very important.

In OC&C's experience, if a management team has 'unreasonable' goals but misses them by 10%, this is probably a much better outcome than setting seemingly 'reasonable' goals and exceeding them by 10%.

Nadir Godrej, one of the two brothers who head Godrej Industries, one of India's leading companies, asks: 'Is a 26% compound growth rate bold enough for you? That's our goal for the next decade. And we will do it with only 5% increase in our headcount and while at the same time becoming carbon neutral.' Now that does seem bold!

Although, it seems that this is par for the course in India. Sumit Chandwani, formerly one of ICICI's talented in-house private equity team in the 'noughties', told me of the ambitious bets they have placed. In 2003 they bought into a cinema business that had only two cinemas – now it has 200. They also backed a water treatment business in 2004 with a turnover of $20m which was being neglected by its Swiss owner. It now boasts an amazing $300m turnover and a truly international footprint.

6 Asking the 'impossible/impolitic' questions

This type of questioning is subtly different from challenge. It is not saying the strategy is wrong but it strikes a more fundamental chord. Depending on the industry and the circumstances, it will be necessary to ask some very difficult questions. So difficult that only the CEO and the top leadership team have the authority to ask them, and to 'give permission' for them to be raised and debated openly.

They include:

> 'What gives us a right to exist?'

'If a competitor were going to challenge us aggressively, what are the three things they could do to us?' – originally asked by Jim Muehlbauer, former CFO at Best Buy.

'What is plan B if this investment, market entry, strategy, etc. fails?'

'Why will we fail?' – the pre-mortem question

As Steve Page, former CFO of UTC, says: 'You need to learn what you do not know so that you can take risks without betting the shop.' And indeed sometimes someone has to stand up and say, 'Our strategy is not working – it is time for a change.' Sir Nigel Rudd, Chairman of BAA and Invensys, advises: 'Have the confidence to change strategy when necessary. Be realistic and bite the bullet.'

7 Choice

In any strategy process there will be times when data, analysis and logic may not give you the answer or even a sensible hint at it. At these times, a choice will have to be made or an assumption adopted. It is important that the CEO and top management is party to that choice – and they often may even need to make it if, in its own right, the choice will effectively define the ultimate strategy. This level of criticality cannot be and should not be delegated.

At different times, it will be the application of an appropriate amount of risk aversion, as Luke Jensen, Group Development Director at J. Sainsbury, suggests: 'Be bold in your thinking but practical in your choices.' Sometimes, it will be necessary for the CEO or someone in

'Be bold in your thinking and practical in your choices.'

the leadership team to step in and to opine about what seems to them to be common sense.

Strategy processes can get bogged down and at that stage it will be incumbent on the CEO to intervene to break the logjam. Cees 't Hart, CEO of FrieslandCampina, notes that the CEO and senior management need 'an iron discipline NOT to take every piece of information into account. Sometimes a judgement just needs to be made.' RBS Board Non-Executive Director Penny Hughes agrees on the need for decisive action at crucial periods: 'Where there are fundamental market shifts afoot, it is better to be early than late.'

Finally there is also the issue that was pointed out to us by a number of people including John Goodwin, CFO of The LEGO Group: 'Strategy is all about choice which also includes stopping some things.' This was echoed by Steve Page of UTC: 'You have to say no in strategy debates with management, not just yes.' As Guilherme Loureiro, former Head of Corporate Strategy at Unilever, says: 'Good strategy is a combination of prioritizing outcomes driven from excellent insight and deciding, as a consequence, what not to do.' There are many tough decisions that are incumbent upon the CEO and the top talent in a company to make.

By fully participating in debates about:

- the uncertainties in the company's environment and thus what the assumptions should be when setting strategy;
- the options which the company could pursue and the pros and cons of each;
- the chosen option and why it is preferred; and
- the elaboration of the chosen option and the route map to achieve the communications programme both internally and externally,

the CEO and top leadership can fundamentally impact the importance with which the process is viewed. If the staff know that the CEO and the key staff around them care about the quality of the process then there is a good chance that they will make sure it is a quality process. Self-interest remains a very good motivating tool.

* * *

The above list of potential interventions may seem onerous, but they're essential if the CEO and the leadership team are going to lead the process of developing a quality strategy. One important by-product of this is that the CEO and the top management team will then truly own the strategy.

Next, of course, it's their job to ensure that strategy gets executed excellently!

In summary, the CEO and senior management must lead the charge to the promised land of good, long-term business-sustaining, strategy. To do this, they must choose the right people to engage with the strategy process, and be sure that those people are attempting to answer the right question; if the answer comes out as 42 (viz. Douglas Adams' seminal book *Hitchhiker's Guide to the Galaxy*) you know you've got the wrong question.

The CEO's guiding hand may well be needed to provide support in the form of a working hypothesis that can be shot down and rebuilt as something new. Strong quality control of the data used to try to answer the question of 'whither the company's future' is essential: the correct data must be used, and it must be processed rigorously and creatively. It is vital that someone in the top strategy team ensures that the group is being sufficiently radical; often this task falls to the leader, the CEO. It is also the CEO who usually has to ensure that the difficult, impolitic, questions have been raised and addressed. And, it may be that the CEO has to grasp the nettle and make a fundamental choice in strategic direction which, once it has been made, all of the top team will need to fully commit to.

The CEO must lead the charge, must show commitment to the process of determining strategy, and take the top team with them in fully owning the new strategy to take the business forward.

The execution of strategy – the people puzzle

'Never assume that you are cleverer than your employees.' ZHANG RUIMIN, CHAIRMAN, HAIER GROUP

It was not entirely clear that we would ever get to the interview with Mr Zhang.

Over dinner in Shanghai the evening before, my colleague received a call announcing a typhoon was approaching and all flights the next morning had been cancelled. We would therefore not be in time for our mid-morning interview with Mr Zhang. After 30 minutes of frantic telephonic activity over dessert, an option presented itself: getting the 7am train to Qingdao. The only flaw in this plan was that this 'high speed' train would take six and a half hours to get to Qingdao, making us several hours late for our appointment, and there was no guarantee that Mr Zhang would be able to change his diary to meet with us later in the day. We would have to phone his office from the train at 9am to see if he would be kind enough to see us.

We took a risk in getting on the train without the guarantee of an interview, but it was a risk well worth taking. Mr Zhang is a remarkable man who has achieved remarkable things. When he established Haier in 1984 he realized there was much to be done to create a viable and world-class company. And he did it.

He realized early that he would have to radically change the culture of the firm in order to produce products that China and the world would want. And to do so, he employed unconventional techniques, such as on one occasion mustering nearly 800 employees and a large number of sledgehammers to publicly destroy 76 sub-standard fridges, just to demonstrate that poor-quality products were unacceptable. He made his point!

But this was not just a piece of showmanship – it was an important lesson that strategies cannot be implemented without the full-blooded support of the company's people. Mr Zhang's innovative management philosophy – one that has earned him the title 'Godfather of Business' in China – is to emphasize responsibility within self-governing units throughout the company. By flattening the management structure, Mr Zhang encourages employees to be self-motivated, to drive innovation and to focus on creating customer value.

Indeed, Mr Zhang reinforced this when we finally met. 'People are the only asset of a company,' he told me. 'It's our only value added. It is management's job to motivate and empower them.' He sees his role as CEO as that of the 'clockmaker', designing a structure to encourage a proactive corporate culture.

I got a similar message when I went to India. Both Daljit Mirchandani, former Chairman and Managing Director of Ingersoll-Rand India, and Nadir Godrej of Godrej Industries formalized what a lot of others had been saying intuitively. Namely, that the key to unlocking strategy was the mobilization of (the right) people. All the good strategy development in the world was little use if the strategist had not done his or her organizational homework about how it would be implemented – and by whom. They had formalized such thinking in their approaches and processes.

This chapter will allow you to test whether you have paid equal homage to the most scarce strategic resource of all – your people.

Developing good strategy involves a lot of hard work and a degree of precision engineering, but it's not rocket science. The strategy development process itself isn't usually the reason why so many efforts go wrong. Execution is where the problems very often begin. 'Implementation is harder than strategy development,' concurs Cees 't Hart, CEO of FrieslandCampina. 'It requires leadership, courage and communication in equal measure.'

With the average tenure of a CEO dropping by the minute, this is a topic that deserves some attention.

'Money is less of a constraint than people.'

Strategic failure can occur for many reasons. But when we set aside instances in which the wrong strategy has been pursued, a majority of the remaining execution failures come down to the question of how the leadership team arrays the human resources at their disposal. As John Brock, Chairman and CEO of Coca-Cola Enterprises, comments dryly: 'The difference between good and bad strategy is very simple – it's people!'

Luke Jensen, Group Development Director at J. Sainsbury, agrees: 'The planning of human capital deployment is more important than financial budgeting. Money is less of a constraint than people.' This rings true for many of those we interviewed. 'Allocating the money is important, but people decisions and their direction will make or break the strategy,' says Mark Newton-Jones, former CEO of Shop Direct Group. Most of our CEO-level interviewees described mobilizing employees as the single most important determinant of strategic success. In terms of the people puzzle, there is a limited number of prerequisites for success.

In the previous chapters, we argued strongly that the CEO increasingly had to lead the strategy development process. More obviously the CEO needs to lead the implementation of strategy. But, if it is mostly about people, then what does he or she need to pay attention to in that respect?

We believe that there are three key strands which relate to people and which, if you get them wrong, will undermine the implementation of strategy:

- **Organizing for success** – getting the right people on the team and organizing them effectively.
- **Leadership** – choosing and implementing strategy requires clarity from the top.
- **Communications and engagement** – strategy needs to be communicated in a compelling way for it to be effective.

You will notice that we have avoided mention of the 'C' word – culture. This is because we believe that, while all companies have a culture and it can be either a liability or an asset for a CEO, it is in the long term an outcome of a company's strategy not a predeterminant of it. It is not an end in itself. Culture is the accumulation of the behaviour of the company employees. If you want to change culture, you have to change a lot of behaviours.

Fritz Oesterle, the former CEO of the international pharmaceuticals wholesaler Celesio, underlines this point. 'Culture can either enable or disable the implementation of strategy,' he says. A deep understanding of the company's existing culture will tell you whether it is an asset or a liability for the strategy you wish to execute. If it's a liability, you're in for a long haul: cultural change is not a rapid process in large organizations.

In the remainder of this chapter, we're going to look at the team, leadership and communications issues in depth.

Organizing for success

Here's how Daljit Mirchandani, former Chairman and Managing Director of Ingersoll-Rand India, described his ideal two-stage strategy process.

- **Stage 1** involved what most of us would recognize as the standard strategy development process adopted by most companies: the sensible consideration of the fundamental issues leading into the design of a forward-looking strategic plan.
- **Stage 2** was unique (or in my experience, very nearly unique). Mirchandani called it the 'Human Capital Strategy' process, and describes it as at least as important as Stage 1.

During Stage 2, the goals and aspirations of the strategic plan were translated into people and organization requirements including capabilities and competences. Existing managers were assessed against these requirements and either confirmed in their posts, given appropriate training or support, or were moved to where their skills would be more useful (or, in some cases, persuaded to leave). Where necessary, managers with the right skills for each critical role were moved from elsewhere in the firm or recruited from outside.

It's certainly true that issues of succession, incentives, talent management and retention are all crucial in strategy implementation. If you do not have such plans, then you put the strategy at risk. You run the risk of operating with the wrong people in poorly defined roles. Getting the right roles and the right people is critical to the execution of the strategy.

'Talent (or the lack of it) in management is one of those issues that frequently gets fumbled,' says Jim Muehlbauer, CFO of Best

Buy. John Goodwin, former CFO of The LEGO Group, agrees: 'Capabilities are the major constraint on strategy. People issues almost always get short-changed in terms of management attention.' Jørgen Buhl Rasmussen, CEO of Carlsberg, could not agree more: 'Strategic planning should deal more explicitly with people issues. Their resolution makes or breaks strategy.'

In our view it is surprising that more companies do not follow Daljit Mirchandani's two-stage process. It seems obvious to us that you need to align your organization with the strategy and then populate it with the right people if you wish to implement your strategy successfully. 'Success comes from execution, which means having the right people and organization in place,' says Jean-François Palus, Deputy CEO of PPR. 'The two questions I always ask are: who will do it? And do we have the right people for it?' Tom Hall, Head of Media for Apax, views the two elements as being inexorably interwoven: 'Management choices should be driven by strategic choices. You will not know who you will need until you have chosen your strategy.' Marcelo Bahia Odebrecht, Chairman of Odebrecht, one of Brazil's biggest corporations, puts it this way: 'When I think of strategy, I do not immediately think of businesses but people. The strategy of our 16 businesses depends entirely on the leaders of those businesses and the opportunities that they see.'

Before moving on to the issue of leadership, one final tip about talent management: eliminate hierarchy wherever possible. The CEO and senior management need to be as near as possible to the coalface, enhancing the speed and quality of decision-making.

Leadership

There are reams of literature on this topic. I am sure that they are very worthy but in our opinion they often miss some rather practical points, like what does the CEO and the executive team do in order to ensure that the strategy is followed? We and our CEO interviewees have a number of pointers that will enhance the likelihood of success. In fact, there are three of them: the Conspiracy Theory of Management, going for gold and clearing the decks.

The Conspiracy Theory of Management

If a CEO wishes to implement his or her strategy single-mindedly, then he is best served by working closely with a small coterie of 'believers' in the immediate executive team. This small team of no more than three or four colleagues/co-conspirators must:

- Believe in the strategy at least as strongly as the CEO.
- Be loyal to the CEO and the company.
- Behave in line with the strategy.
- Be willing to explain the strategy (and its implications) to doubters.

'You absolutely need a guiding coalition of [two or three] top people who can huddle with the CEO to get things done,' says Sandy Ogg, a seasoned HR professional and Operating Partner with Blackstone.

The value of this 'conspiracy' cannot be overestimated.

Being a CEO is generally very lonely. The well-being of the company is the CEO's responsibility, yet it is very difficult to get unfiltered and unbiased feedback. The CEO alone calls the shots, including deciding whether executives remain employed. Clearly, this makes it very difficult for the team to disagree with the CEO, or to offer constructive challenge.

One solution involves fostering a sense of trust and joint

endeavour with a handful of close colleagues. And we really are talking about a handful: not ten, or 12, and certainly not the entire executive committee. Here's why:

- The creation of trust requires investment in the individual and the CEO does not have infinite time to invest.
- The co-conspirators need to believe that they are special and that their relationship with the CEO is preferential. They need to become an inner cabinet, trusted lieutenants in the noble deed of taking the company forward. Importantly, they should also be able to challenge the CEO behind closed doors, precisely because the CEO trusts them.
- They need to feel empowered by, but also responsible to, the CEO for the implementation of a vision. Only a limited number of executives can properly feel responsible for this.

'Management conspiracy is clearly necessary to implement strategy,' says Steve Page, former CFO of UTC. As Gavin Darby, former CEO of Premier Foods, observes: 'You need the team populated with a few true believers.' John Goodwin, CFO of The LEGO Group, agrees: 'You need no more than four co-conspirators who really get it.' The top team has the freedom to disagree with the strategy before it is formed, but must commit to it entirely once it has been signed off. To quote Romulo de Mello Dias, CEO of Cielo: 'The management conspiracy allows you to communicate openly and even disagree but once the decision is taken then you have to fall in line. The top team has to follow only one direction.'

This team leads the implementation of strategy. If the CEO is not in the room when strategy comes up then one of the co-conspirators will be able to point the rest of the people in the right direction and show them what appropriate behaviours are.

Going for gold

Attracting solid gold performers also increases the likelihood of success. Indeed, many of our CEO interviewees insisted on the importance of (over) investing in people. Hire the best, train them well, challenge them frequently and take risks by promoting them early. You will almost always be rewarded by superior commitment and performance. As Carlos Medeiros, CEO of BRMALLS, says: 'The CEO's major impact in a company is related to people – attracting the best and creating the culture and values which will allow them to out-perform. Excellent people produce excellent results.'

'You need smarter, more educated managers nowadays in order to match competitors who are increasingly well informed, capable,' says Gavin Darby. This is particularly the case in India, says Daljit Mirchandani, former Chairman and Managing Director of Ingersoll-Rand India, where development of people is key. 'Human capital strategy is crucial,' he stresses. 'At Ingersoll, we were very proactive about investing in people and their training.' David Feffer, Chairman of Suzano, puts it simply: 'Good people will deliver good results; excellent people will deliver excellent ones. The CEO's major task therefore is to find the excellent people.' Jørgen Buhl Rasmussen, CEO of Carlsberg, agrees: 'Strategically, getting the best people is the top priority.'

Clearing the decks

The corollary of Management Conspiracy is a need to expunge confirmed doubters. As Duncan Painter, CEO of Top Right Group, notes, 'People are the reason that businesses fail. You should always make an effort to bring dissenters into the fold, but if this fails, remove them.' Their potentially cynical attitude towards a strategy in which they don't believe will become toxic. It will make implementation more difficult and costly than it otherwise would have been.

'People are the reason that businesses fail.'

The doubter is a poor role model for his or her juniors, creating scepticism that radiates out and downwards through the ranks of the company.

'If your top team doesn't act as a team then replace it,' says Ian Livingston, CEO of BT Group. 'And make a large part of their bonus reliant on shared goals to drive home the importance of collaboration.' Arno Mahlert, former CEO and CFO of maxingvest, agrees: 'Managers need to create the right culture by being true role models. They need to inspire credibility by being open to feedback. They also need to tolerate some mistakes. But the one thing that cannot be tolerated is destructive behaviour.'

'Strategy development needs openness and challenge,' says John Brock, Chairman and CEO of Coca-Cola Enterprises. 'But once the strategy is set, you have to execute, execute, execute. You cannot afford nay-sayers.' Rob van den Bergh of NV Deli Universal concurs: 'If someone is not aligned, you need to get them off the pitch.'

They may be good, smart and effective at some things but if they are getting in the way of the execution of the strategy then it is critical to remove them. Sometimes you can move people to less critical roles. At its most extreme, you may find it necessary to manage a few high-profile dismissals, getting rid of executives who do not 'get it' and cannot go with the flow.

From time to time, one has to make observations that others may find unpalatable. This is one of those moments. During our conversations with CEOs we asked the question as to where human resources stands in terms of being the key adviser to the CEO – i.e. one of the co-conspirators – when it comes to the people issues mentioned above. We were saddened, but not totally surprised, by their rather depressing responses.

We have argued above that people make or break a strategy. It would seem logical, therefore, that HR should have a seat at the 'conspiratorial' table – however, this is seldom true. HR professionals seemingly do not embrace formal and informal people issues as part of their role. They should know who is great and who is less good, who is up to it or not, who is a team player, etc. – but they don't! And it is not obvious why …

Here is a selection of comments on the role of HR professionals, from CEOs who, for obvious reasons, would prefer to remain anonymous:

- 'Senior HR (and IT) people are not involved at the higher echelons of the team; they are too specialized. They are critical on the one hand, but blinkered on the other.'
- 'My human capital strategy is to have a really commercially savvy HR guy, not some HR super-specialist. I need someone who can work out what we need to deliver the strategy and whether we have got it and what to do about it. Same with IT!'
- 'Human capital strategy is a key component of the overall strategy. I do not need HR specialists for this. I need commercial people with some HR skills.'
- 'HR is underpotentialized. Too detail-oriented and not focused on mission critical competences, where the relevant questions are these: do we have them and if not, how do we get them? We need business people in charge of HR!'

Clearly the business of human capital management provokes a lot of frustration – so much so that some of the CEOs we interviewed suggested that the phrase 'human resources' has become so devalued that its use should be prohibited. Now, as always, the real issue is something we might call people or talent management.

And senior HR professionals should concentrate less on the pension rights of employees and more on whether the company has the right employees and, if not, what they are going to suggest to the CEO be done about it. Gary Lubner, CEO of Belron, summarizes this neatly: 'HR should be given to someone that understands people, not just employees – usually not an HR specialist but someone with a broader grasp of the commercial realities of the company.'

Communications and engagement

Communications. It sounds pretty straightforward, doesn't it? But in our experience that's the last thing it is.

Communication (i.e. talking the talk) is half art, half science. The element of science involves deciding what you say, and to whom. The art of communication is all about how you say it – in a compelling and collegiate way. Without good communications, engagement is unlikely!

Let's deal with the science first.

Strategy needs to be communicated in a number of different ways according to the audience. In the interests of simplicity, here are four examples of different constituencies:

1. **The co-conspirators:** they need to know everything about the strategy so that they can talk the talk without even having to think about it. Your co-conspirators will be the role models for many others. In the context of day-to-day operations, they will advocate the strategy once the CEO has left the room.

2. **The executive:** the rest of the senior team will need to have the strategy explained in some detail. They will need to know why it is the best alternative. They will also need to have the implications spelled out for them. What is the strategy's endgame? What represents winning behaviour at all levels in the company? What is appropriate activity (and equally important, what is not)? What is the investment strategy? Internally, who are the winners and the losers? How should the 'losers' be incentivized? Goals need to be communicated.
3. **Management:** managers need to understand the strategy and why it is right. More importantly, they need to understand what they must do to make sure their part of the empire does its bit. What is expected of them?
4. **Frontline teams:** employees need to have the strategy explained to them simply and in terms of what it means to them. It needs to be explained to them in terms of its purpose. Most essentially they need to understand the importance of what they are doing and how it makes a difference. If you can engage the hearts and minds of frontline employees, then the probability of successfully executing the strategy will increase disproportionately.

The nature of communication is fundamentally different at each of these levels. Needless to say, a single webcast by the CEO is not enough. As Rick Hamada, CEO of Avnet, Inc., says: 'The single biggest illusion regarding communication is that it has occurred.'

At OC&C, we are great believers in the Ripple Theory of Engagement, which sees a core message filter out in stages from a central determination of strategy by the CEO and his or her co-conspirators to a list of clear action points for those on the front lines.

The Ripple Theory of Communication

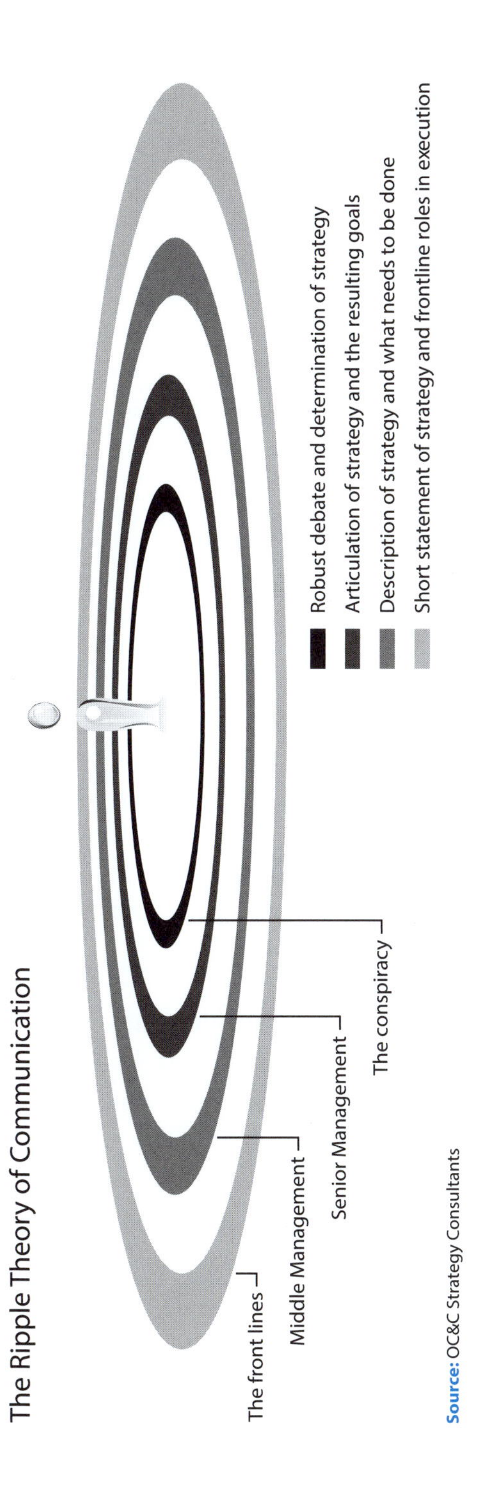

Source: OC&C Strategy Consultants

Here's the approach adopted by Pedro Pereira da Silva, CEO of Biedronka, the Polish supermarket chain: 'We communicate "hard strategy" to the top three to five people. The management conspiracy implied by this is key. We then communicate a softer version of the strategy to the top 250 managers.'

Tim Steiner, CEO of Ocado, has similar views. 'Once the CEO has chosen a strategy he needs to explain it to his top team and then communicate it widely, frequently and well to the wider team.'

The further out you go from the inner sanctum of the conspirators, the more you need to craft the message into a simple, attractive, engaging and relevant communication. 'Strategy must be boiled down to manageable bites if it is to be effective,' says Sandy Ogg, Operating Partner in private equity group Blackstone. But it must be communicated to everyone in the organization. 'It is absolutely essential to the execution of strategy,' says Laura Karet, CEO of Giant Eagle, 'that you get engagement all the way from the "inner cabinet" to the cashier in a shop!'

'We should not try to "academize" strategy,' says former Celesio CEO Dr Fritz Oesterle. 'In the end, it is not an exact science but the definition of how to get from A to B.'

This is where the art comes in. Working out how to engage people and motivate them is not easy: it's at this point that authenticity and simplicity come into their own. All (good) strategy can be reduced to one sheet of paper: it should be easy enough to avoid over-complication. But communicating in an authentic way is a job for the individual CEO: only he or she can gauge what will resonate within the company.

'You need to get strategy on to one page. If something is not on the page, then it is not strategically important,' says Phil Bentley, the former CEO of British Gas.

* * *

So talent management, leadership and communication/ engagement are, in our opinion, the keys to solving the people puzzle. Again, all these facets of the riddle can only be addressed by the CEO. If you fail to think hard about what you want from people and how you intend to get it, you will regrettably get what you deserve – a mediocre implementation of your strategy.

In summary, a business stands or falls because of its people. Our CEOs were united in their belief that the most important task of any CEO in any business is to choose the right people for the top management team. They should not only be excellent, but also be complementary to the skills of the CEO and of each other. This jigsaw puzzle of matching skills with needs is the most vital weapon in the CEO's armoury for business success.

Achieving it requires three things. First, organizing for success is about choosing the right people and organizing them effectively. Second, choosing and implementing good strategy requires clarity from the top, often this is best achieved by use of the Conspiracy Theory of Management, whereby a CEO is surrounded by a loyal coterie of true believers in the strategy, who act in line with the strategy and can explain it to doubters. As a corollary to this, a CEO should pursue the best talent and not be afraid to lose people who cannot, or will not, align with the strategy. Last, and by no means least, the strategy needs to be effectively communicated to each and every person in the company – a 'Ripple' method which reaches each level in the business in a way which is relevant to them.

It is vital that hard thinking is done about what you want from your people and how you intend to get it, in order that your strategy can be fully implemented.

6

So how do managers make a difference to strategy?

'Strategy has to be clear and simple and then communicated consistently, steadily and frequently.' MIKE WALSH, CEO, LEXISNEXIS LEGAL& PROFESSIONAL

Strategy does not implement itself.

As you will have noted by now, the overwhelming view from our CEOs is that rubber hits the road when strategy meets execution. This is where the boys (girls) are sorted from the men (women). Unless the whole company is mobilized then full, single-minded and timely implementation of strategy is unlikely. Indeed if the team is not all pulling (or pushing) in the same direction then it is likely that some will be pulling (or pushing) in the opposite direction with the likelihood that little progress will be made. Worse still they may be following their own agenda with the result they will be pulling in all sorts of directions.

'Alignment of management and employees to strategy is the single biggest differentiator between good strategy and bad strategy', observes Michael Hansen, CEO of Cengage, the distance learning company. And as Mike White, CEO of DIRECTV says: 'It is increasingly difficult to have a distinct proprietary strategy so execution is critical.' He goes on to say: 'I'll take great execution over great strategy any time.'

Strategy is a zero sum game: if you are going nowhere strategically and your competitors have got their acts together then, by definition, your firm will be going backwards. Getting the management fully aligned and committed is thus a cornerstone of good strategy execution. This is often a much neglected task!

But how do you achieve alignment to, and better still, ownership of, the strategy by the management team (usually hundreds, if not thousands, of people) and, better still, build it into an unstoppable tsunami of competitive superiority through outstanding execution?

General exhortations to management on the strategy and its importance will not get you there. Furthermore, you cannot achieve it by bringing hundreds into the strategy formulation/development task; as we have heard earlier, you can only involve so many people in the strategy process if you want to have a hope of coming out the other end with a clean crisp strategy.

Ultimately, the manager's role is to manage their part of the business and not the overall business – that's what the leadership team is there for. Sure, they will welcome a bit of context which helps them feel a member of the wider team. But what they really need is a relatively simple interpretation of the strategy that will help them understand what *they* can do to make a difference and why making a difference is a worthwhile activity.

'Strategy is all about the higher purpose' says Barney Harford, CEO of Orbitz Worldwide. 'What will the enduring impact of the business be?' It is vital that strategy can be distilled to something simple and communicable.

Management need to understand:

- What the strategy is in simple terms, and the purpose that it encompasses.
- How the function of management or its role fits into that.
- What they need to do to support the strategy … and what they need to stop doing!
- How you will know whether they are doing what they committed to do.

- How they will be rewarded for achieving it (not just in monetary terms!).

To achieve this understanding without transfixing the organization in 'process' requires a combination of the Management Conspiracy Theory and the Ripple Theory of Communications/Engagement, as expounded in Chapter 5. To quote Geoff Molson, President and CEO of Club de Hockey Canadien: 'Strategy is often words on a piece of paper – that is no longer good enough. You need a vision and then strategy is how you deliver it.'

In essence, you need to engage management in the need for future thinking, foster a sense of belief in each of them about the strategy in terms of where the company is going and why, and mobilize them for their part in delivering the agreed strategy. As Richard Rankin, CEO of ACH Food Companies, notes: 'Strategy is not the same as planning. Strategy is all about how we are going to compete. Most companies are hungry for strategy.'

Bill Rogers, CEO of SunTrust Banks, Inc., echoes this: 'The engagement process needs to start with trying to answer the question – why are we here, what is our role in the world? I never use the word strategy when talking to my teammates. There is no surer way of losing their interest! The job of the CEO is to bring clarity to complexity and purpose to the work of the team.' Doug Tough, CEO of International Flavors & Fragrances, agrees: '"Purpose" is bubbling up more and more in conversations about "why do I work here?" and CEOs need to be able to describe it without hesitation.'

In the 'enabling/empowering leadership' model of management, execution is a team endeavour. Decided by the top team, shared with management and executed together as a shared task. As Sascha Bopp, CEO of Crate and Barrel, says: 'The Management

Conspiracy is an important concept – unless your key execs are totally in synch you lose a lot of time, and engagement.' This is a company led from the top but not 100% dependent on the CEO for both the creation and the execution of strategy. Think Richard Branson, the unquestioned leader of the Virgin Group, who famously says that he delegates almost all of his business to his team.

Indeed, if you cannot make strategy execution a team endeavour then your strategy is in real trouble. Dogs smell fear they say. Similarly, if one of the management team displays off-strategy behaviour that is not then corrected decisively, then bad habits will spread fast.

The best way to engage management is to think of them all as potential senior leaders and therefore consider them as equals who can substantially self-determine their actions/behaviours but they need to understand the context within which they are operating, what they need to be doing and why, and what outcomes are expected.

'It is the CEO's job to give the team the confidence to do their job,' says Chris Weston of Direct Energy. Above all management need to understand the definition of what success looks like. As Brian Newman, Senior Vice-President of Strategy and Finance for PepsiCo, says: 'Strategy is not just an analytical outcome of a process. It needs to be emotionally owned otherwise it will not get executed.'

Most employees want to go home in the evening thinking they have done a good, worthwhile job and hence if you give them the opportunity to shine, and recognize good performance in them, then half the battle of engagement is won. This speaks to the importance of purpose and how this is an increasingly important element underpinning strategy execution. 'Just making money is not enough – you need to give employees a sense of cause and purpose,' opines Michael Hansen of Cengage Learning.

To quote Sir Richard Branson, one of the best ways to grow a business is by 'hiring excellent people who believe in your company and share your goals, and then by helping them to learn and improve their skills. This isn't optional: If your best people aren't growing in their careers as your business gains traction and expands, they will quickly lose enthusiasm for their work. And before you know it, you'll be dealing with unsatisfied customers as well as unsatisfied employees.'[1]

Don Knauss, CEO of Clorox, agrees: 'You need to put "people" even before the shareholders. If you don't then you will have nothing to talk to the shareholders about.' As Mike Walsh, CEO of LexisNexis Legal & Professional, puts it: 'You have to have a really embedded strategy process – everyone in the organization needs to see what is going on and therefore what their role is in the delivery of the strategy.'

The case study of Burberry is a good example of how to mobilize a team to implement a changed strategy and turn a business around. Burberry was a mid-sized stable business in the luxury clothing market in which there were a number of well-established businesses accounting for a large percentage of market share as well as many niche players. Led by Rose Marie Bravo, who was appointed CEO in 1997, the new top team had concluded that the company had completely underplayed the strength and positioning of their potentially very valuable heritage brand and had become stuck in terms of competing on only a range of fixed clothing lines. They were not competing on value, but were also not expanding in the premium range. The outcome: they were losing share to a variety of players without any reason for the downward spiral to change. The new top team was in a hurry both to stop the increasingly obvious decline of the brand in the short term as well as to build a valuable business for the long term.

Consumer research was undertaken to find out how the company was really positioned. And consumers thought a lot of good things such as that Burberry had high brand name recognition, with an assurance of consistency in the quality and durability of products, a strong image that was seen as synonymous with quality, style and elegance. In fact, there was not much wrong with consumer perception and acceptability of the brand and the product. The problem was that the customers were largely older males and, in the UK shops, Asian tourists; 75% of sales were accounted for by the Far East. In addition, by the 1990s Burberry had lost substantial control over its licencees with the result that the price, quality and designs varied across markets.

In other words, there was a major opportunity to reverse the decline by reorganizing the company to produce global consistency, and leveraging the quality associations of the heritage brand with clothes designs and products that would appeal to a younger target market while working off the traditional British craftsmanship perceptions of the brand. The goal was to rebrand Burberry from an outdated outerwear manufacturer to a luxury lifestyle brand. Bravo's strategy to reinvent the classic British brand and sell the message globally included signing top model Kate Moss and recruiting the young designer Christopher Bailey, greatly increasing the line of products, including launching Burberry perfumes, and reorganizing the company structure.

But how to get the management to accept all these changes and behave as though they were brand winners given that they had had years of being inculcated into seeing the brand as historic and unchanging?

Not easy, but achievable. Three steps were required:

1. ***Communication***

   By sharing the market and consumer research with the senior and middle management the potential of the brand could be seen in short order. In addition it was clear that the positioning of the brand and products had been inappropriate to generate growth.

2. ***Description of the end game***

   Rather than telling managers what to do, the top team spent time telling them the general outcomes that the strategy needed to achieve. Where should the brand be positioned? Where will it be the number one? Which new products should the brand encompass? What will the price realization per unit be? What will the overall market share be? How will consumers perceive the product? Why will they be able to beat competition?

3. ***Which levers to pull***

   As argued above, in most industries, managers do not need to be told what their jobs are. Rather they need to be told what they need to be aiming for.

Goal-oriented communications are critical in this process. And this is where the Conspiracy Theory comes in. At each level in the company a core team of key influencers needs to be brought together to commit to a series of goals – probably led by a 'primus inter pares' – and agree what they as a team will try to achieve to make the strategy happen. These teams need to be talking together so that action across functions is consistent and complementary. 'Strategy is about transformational thinking – how can we move the levers to improve the business?' says Brian Newman, Senior Vice-President of Strategy and Finance of PepsiCo.

To progress through these three steps the enabling/ empowering leadership model of management is needed, because the steps require a degree of collective responsibility and autonomy/ self-determination for them to work. This autonomy required of management should be reflected through the appraisal system where soft criteria such as trust, collaboration, integrity, honesty, reliability and initiative should be held in high esteem. These qualities are difficult to measure, but you know them when you 'see' them.

As Marcelo Bahia Odebrecht, Chairman of Odebrecht says: 'A business works well when you have created a culture of trust, shared reward, and reinvestment which can then thrive on client focus, delegation and sustainability.' Don Knauss, CEO of the Clorox Company, puts it starkly: 'You need to add integrity, curiosity, optimism, compassion and humility into the appraisal criteria for executives. Without these values they will fail in today's world.'

In the case of Burberry, Rose Marie Bravo and her team increased Burberry revenues of £428m in 2001, to £995m in 2008. An astonishing turnaround. As of 2012, Burberry has total revenues of £1.8bn.

However, the enabling/empowering leadership model of management is not the only model. Its polar opposite also exists: the autocratic model of management. This model may operate in a company despite normal management structures. It is a function of the CEO's style, not the company's structure.

In such companies, you are fine if you have a leader who has the right sort of vision which will carry the company through despite a lack of management participation. Think Steve Jobs at Apple. On the other hand if you have an autocratic leader and their vision is not right then, at some point, the house of cards is likely to come crashing down. Think Leona Helmsley, who ruled over the employees in her hotel chain with a rod of iron, until disgruntled employees successfully raised charges of tax evasion and extortion against her and the Queen of Mean had to spend two years in prison.

Mobilizing management in the autocratic model requires a little more 'smoke and mirrors' and is fundamentally premised on the success of the leader. The management team are not usually privy to the plans and ultimate aims of the strategy – indeed, the autocratic leader sometimes may not have fully grasped these themselves and instead be operating on instinct. Rather, the managers are incentivized by success and by proximity to their powerful leader.

Neither type/style of management is necessarily right or wrong, but without doubt the board is taking a bigger risk with the autocratic model as it is similar to placing all your roulette chips on one number (in this case the 'number' is the CEO). Great if the number comes up, but you lose all if you have made the wrong choice.

A good way of thinking about the role of management in strategy execution is to think in geographic terms:

- **North** – what interactions are important to ***a manager's seniors***?
- **East/West** – how should the manager deal with ***their own job and their peer group***?
- **South** – how should managers guide ***their direct reports***?

North

On a day-to-day basis, the manager is responsible for executing against the objectives set with their boss in operational terms – tasks, deadlines, metrics, etc. But, in terms of the manager's role in strategy some more subtle forces are in play, and managers have two key roles to fulfil.

First, management has a critical role to play in terms of helping their seniors to understand what is going on strategically – the middle management of the company is typically aware of changes on the ground before the top leadership team. So, management has a duty to feed upwards observations about:

- What is happening to consumers – are they changing their habits?
- What is happening to competitors – are they feeding off some inherent competitive advantage that we had not previously noticed?
- Our performance – are we winning enough business or are we systematically weak?

When these communications reach the senior echelons, they will form an important part of the company's situation analysis. What is needed, says Barney Harford, CEO of Orbitz, are: 'T-people – people who go deep in their areas of speciality, but also have the curiosity to go broad in developing their understanding of the rest of the company. That's the kind of person who can help make connections between different parts of the organization that are so critical to a company's success. To nurture T-people, you need to be super proactive about sharing information about what different groups within the company are up to. That's when you really see the magic happen.' According to Paul Todd, Vice-President of Strategy for Marketplaces at eBay: 'Strategy is about clarity and insight. While strategy has not changed, the way we get insight has.'

Another C-suite interviewee concurs: 'Companies need more bottom up strategy, more feedback loops, more information about what is happening at the front end of the business to reflect the fact that strategy is increasingly about many smaller, more discrete decisions being taken closer to the market.'

Of course, it is vital that the correct tone is struck for these communications: they need to be constructive and evidence based. Observations which are anecdotal or defensive can be interpreted as threats to the strategy. But observations from management are vital to leadership efficiency. As Mike White, CEO of DIRECTV, says: 'Always look for blind spots, try to know what you do not know. Be a student of your company.' Phil Bentley, Managing Director of British Gas, advises: 'You need to go out and talk to the frontline people, investors and employees. The answers are usually "in the room" they are just not known!' As Laura Karet, CEO of Giant Eagle, puts it: 'It is critical to put in place feedback loops which allow people to tell you the hard truths about "where the bad stuff is".'

The second critical role for managers is to be creative and suggest ways in which the execution of the strategy could be improved upon or made more efficient. Managers should be encouraged to come forward with options for improvement in process or content and incentivized for such proposals. Don Knauss, CEO of Clorox, says: 'You need to create a culture where middle management can challenge the core processes even though you do not want them to be challenging the strategy every day of the week.' Sir George Buckley, former CEO of 3M, agrees: 'Given that people are essential to the execution of strategy, you need to create an environment in which trust, self-belief and common sense are prevalent in all their forms.'

Clearly, these critical roles cannot be carried out without sympathetic and receptive ears in senior management. Even though there is often a need for a CEO to decide between choices, seek alignment and move forward, this need for decisiveness is not the same as autocracy. Autocracy will kill feedback loops and creativity in a heartbeat.

East/West

Collaboration and trust are key variables in how managers conduct themselves horizontally with their peers. Often they are essentially in competition with their peers as they want to progress through the company as rapidly as possible and that does regrettably involve being chosen in front of the next person.

What is important though is that the style of behaviour to be inculcated in management is one of teamwork being better than 'being a sole-trader', that helping others succeed is better for the company rather than standing to one side and watching them and the company fail. As Jeff Holzschuh, Chairman of Institutional Securities Group at Morgan Stanley, says: 'Collaboration between units is increasingly critical. We all need to build it into our core business models.'

In addition, managers should be encouraged to give themselves time to think fundamentally about their role, their major activities, and the reports they generate, and how both can be improved. Harnessing such creativity from 'those who know' is critical to the continuous improvement of the business.

South

Managers have as much responsibility for setting the corporate tone as the CEO and leadership. Their behaviour, actions and style will materially influence those reporting to them. You definitely 'reap what you sow' in this respect. It is certainly a case of 'do unto others what you would have done unto you'.

Helping your immediate reports to define what good looks like, measuring their output, encouraging them to do better, setting goals, being receptive to new inputs and improvements are all critical to the role of management, and ultimately to the propagation and execution of strategy.

As noted in Chapter 5, the CEOs we consulted in the researching of this book were unanimous that it is the task of the CEO to choose the top management team. Sascha Bopp, CEO of Crate and Barrel, states: 'The one thing you should never delegate is the recruitment of the top team. Make the first call, do the first interview, select the right headhunter – it is a necessary and high return investment.' Chris Weston, CEO of Direct Energy, puts it succinctly: 'The CEO's main task is to get the right team and to align them with strategy.' Greg Parker, CEO of the Parker Companies, concurs: 'The CEO needs the right team to help him with the strategy. The CEO's role is then to help that team do better.'

Our CEOs were also unanimous that you should be seeking not just talent, but world-class talent. According to Phil Bentley, Managing Director of British Gas: '"Can't afford them" is never a good reason for not employing the best.' Rick Smith, CEO of Equifax, agrees: 'If you are really committed to your strategy then you need to make sure you already have (or bring in) world-class talent.' Above all, you should ensure your top team are completely committed to the strategy, as Michael Polk, CEO of Newell Rubbermaid, says: 'When the top team are not invested in the strategy it leads to a lack of confidence that they could really execute and hence it is probably better that they go.'

While it is important to contain the strategy defining process to a small tight group of people, it is equally important to widen the net so all management are involved in the execution of strategy and, where necessary, provide the impetus from the frontline to modify the strategy. Without their participation the company will, in terms of strategy, be flying blind.

* * *

In summary, strategy is like a soufflé – the recipe is straightforward, its chances of success are all in the execution.

In order for your management to effectively implement your strategy they need to understand several things: what the strategy is in simple terms, and the purpose that it encompasses, how their role fits into that, what they need to do on a day-to-day basis to support the strategy, how you will know whether they are doing that, and how they will be rewarded for achieving it, both monetarily and otherwise. To achieve a strategic turnaround, once the strategy has been devised it must be communicated effectively so that at each level managers can ensure that every member of the company understands their role in executing it, from the top team to the frontline.

One way to communicate the strategy to managers so they can enact upon it, is to focus on the end game – if you are clear about where the company is going long term, managers can see more easily where their role fits in with that. The aim is to reach an understanding regarding which levers to pull in the business to change its direction. A useful way to think about the role that managers should fulfil is in terms of the compass: managers need to communicate and ensure strategy is executed, both South to people below them, and to East and West with their manager peers. They also need to communicate changes (in business environments, consumer behaviour or the company's progress) North, to the CEO.

7

Ten strategic pitfalls . . .

'Get fired for your own mistakes, not someone else's.' SIR TERRY LEAHY, ADVISER AND FORMER CEO, TESCO

Little did I know when I sat down with two of my partners, James George and David Hosein, that the subject of our relatively light-hearted debate could inspire so much constructive argument. Our major 'day job' preoccupation is with developing strategies to help our clients win. The topic of this conversation was radically different: what stops companies from winning? Indeed, what are the pitfalls that make for strategic failure?

We debated six failings, to which our CEOs, many of whom were keen to see this list of 'deadly sins', have added four more to our already life-threatening catalogue of 'bear traps'.

Here, then, are ten of the most common pitfalls that a senior manager should seek to avoid when making strategy work.

- Excessive short-termism
- Ignoring external trends, particularly challenging ones
- Overconfidence based on existing success
- Failure to respond to structural changes in the market
- Failure to employ the best possible team
- Failure to focus and getting blown off course
- Inability to foster belief in the strategy
- Inability to translate the strategy into a corporate 'purpose' which employees can buy into
- Failure to instil a sense of pace
- Failure to create accountability for results

A leader's ability to avoid pitfalls like these is directly related to the quality and single-mindedness of the top team. If they believe

– and behave – in a way that's consistent with the strategy, then there's a very good chance that these pitfalls can be avoided. But let's understand them in more detail:

1 Excessive short-termism

Most CEOs will claim that they are innocent of this sin. Instead, they will say that short-termism is the fault of the stock market and/or aggressive owners. There's often some truth in such protestations of innocence. As Antonio Carlos Guimarães, CEO of Syngenta Latam, notes, 'A new CEO needs to worry about the short-term results while aiming at the long-term objectives. But there is no future if you don't deliver immediate results.'

Among the 100-plus CEOs we interviewed, many were deeply aware of the short-term demands placed upon quoted companies. 'Beware the quarterly earnings trap,' says Steve Page, former CFO of UTC. 'Reserve your opinion on "guidance" wherever possible. It is downside only and can come back to bite you viciously.'

Even the best-intentioned efforts to keep short-termism at bay by emphasizing long-term objectives can produce unintended consequences. Marks & Spencer, the British retailer, fell into this trap in the late 1990s. The then Chairman and CEO, Richard Greenbury, who was himself a critic of short-termism in the financial markets, announced his aim of becoming the first British retailer to generate annual profits of £1bn. It was an inspiring, relatively short-term, objective, which had the desired effect on the share price. The company achieved its goal in 1998, turning in pre-tax profits of £1.17bn.

Unfortunately there was a high price to pay. As the company geared its operations towards profit, a lack of investment in sales infrastructure – stores, IT, training, etc. – started to erode the company's long-term hold on its markets. Value-based rivals made off with the family silver, undermining M&S's relationship with its traditional customers. A profit warning followed in 1999, and Richard Greenbury was forced to step down. Recovery didn't come easily. It was 2008 before M&S once again delivered a profit of £1bn.

This salutary example suggests that even the most admired CEOs can experience difficulties if they dare to try weaning the market off the drug of short-term performance. On the other hand, there are ways of mitigating the market's apparent addiction. Jack Welch, Chairman and CEO at General Electric between 1981 and 2001, was a past master at managing the trade-off between long-term objectives and short-term expectations.

His long-term vision was radical: it involved moving away from hardware sales and one-off revenues towards services. Yet as soon as Welch started to meet with success, what had once seemed radical quickly became the norm. Finding a way of blending short-term pressures with long-term objectives in this way is essential. As Luis Maroto, President and CEO of Amadeus, the publicly traded company that processes 850 million transactions a year on behalf of the travel industry, told us: 'You've got to combine long-term and short-term perspectives. You must think both ways. It's essential to manage these conflicts.'

With clear and sensible communication, some of this pressure can be relieved. It's worth considering, for example, which parts (or dimensions) of the overall strategy you can share with the market. For example, the pre-announcement of a major restructuring or investment that will pay off in a year or two might be tolerated by the markets if the objectives are clear and seemingly logical. The timing of announcements is important, and so is the ability to manage expectations. As we've already noted, communication is half art and half science: what you don't say in public is at least as important as what you do say.

2 Ignoring external trends

A failure to pay attention to short-term external trends – for instance not properly tracking customer needs and understanding competitor moves – will trip up even the best strategies.

'Strategy is all about forecasting change.'

'Nowadays the world is an uncertain place. The consequences of our actions are much less predictable. Today strategy is all about forecasting change,' says Patrick Boissier, Chairman and CEO of DCNS, a world leader in naval defence and one of Europe's biggest shipbuilders. 'We need to be much more creative, make sense out of weak signals and external change. It is much less comfortable, certainly, but much more fun.' Anthony Hucker, President of Giant Food, agrees: 'Never let a good crisis go to waste – it is always a good opportunity to ask some fundamental home truths.'

Typical of an organization that has paid insufficient attention to trends is Research In Motion, the makers of the pioneering BlackBerry. RIM was, for a few years, the clear market leader in smart technologies, but, alas, no more. RIM's failure to respond to very clear market trends was described by one CBS commentator as 'the modern equivalent of Nero fiddling while Rome burned'. But what was the source of the apparent inactivity of RIM? A number of things contributed to their slide:

- A failure to move beyond their traditional corporate sector and a lack of realization that 'scale' would now be defined as being relevant in both the consumer and the corporate sectors not just in the business market alone. They continued to have a high share of the corporate market, not realizing that Apple and others would get to scale in the consumer sector and then 'come after them' in the corporate market as they are now doing very effectively.

- A failure to innovate in device, functionality and the design of their devices contributed to their lack of appeal. The BlackBerry of today still looks substantially the same as that of five years ago.
- A failure to understand the app market. Only now are they moving to provide a platform compatible with other systems.

The shareholders of RIM should rightly feel short-changed. The writing has been on the wall for some time now and they deserve a lot better. It is a tough market but not that tough.

Coca-Cola also suffered from a mild version of this when they seemingly went out of their way to ignore the influx of the new wave of 'alternative beverages', instead focusing on their heartland of carbonated soft drinks. For instance, they were very late into the energy drinks market and in 2008 had to make up for lost time by entering a distribution agreement with the market leading brand, Monster Energy, owned by Hansen Natural Corporation.

3 Overconfidence based on existing success

You need to be confident to get things done. But equally, overconfidence is a deadly sin, a pitfall lying in wait for the unwary. It often stems from a track record of success in buoyant markets. Eventually, businesses of this kind can start to confuse the effect of being successful in benign conditions with innate effectiveness. 'Deep conviction in a company can sometimes be presumption and possibly even prejudice or ignorance,' says Stuart Fletcher, CEO of Bupa. 'Presumption needs to be questioned regularly and vigorously.' Missing or denying reality is a fatal consequence of lack of honesty or objectivity. John Brock, Chairman and CEO of Coca-Cola Enterprises, is clear that this is a challenge: 'Humans are basically optimistic, but strategy has to confront brutal truths.'

Even in difficult and challenging markets, companies can overestimate the value of their business model, customer base and ways of doing things. As Rainer Hillebrand, Vice-CEO of Otto, puts it: 'Existing customers are an asset as is your business model, but be careful if Amazon, eBay or others start stealing your future customers – youth! You might be tempted to look the other way because overall business performance is adequate.'

The message here is simple: you need to be ruthlessly honest. Otherwise, you may wake up one day and find your business gone. This has been called the 'The Delusion of Absolute Performance' by Phil Rosenzweig in his book *The Halo Effect … and the Eight Other Business Delusions that Deceive Managers*.[1]

Blockbuster is a clear example of a business that failed to move with the times and saw its business model collapse on both sides of the Atlantic. Blockbuster was once the dominant movie rental company in the US and UK, but its DVD rental and return business strategy became increasingly superseded by alternative methods of acquiring and sharing movies, and the attraction of a bricks and mortar venue from which to choose films disappeared to a vanishing point in the younger market. Blockbuster attempted forays into online streaming but it was too little too late to beat off the intense competitive pressure from Netflix, iTunes and Love Film. The company filed for Chapter 11 bankruptcy in America in 2010, and bankruptcy in the UK followed in 2013.

4 Failure to respond to structural changes in the market

Refusing to acknowledge that structural changes are real can also lead to flawed strategic responses. The internet (and all of the new business models that it has enabled) is no more likely to go away than the tide.

Denying that anything other than the current model will work was another one of the delusions noted by Phil Rosenzweig. He called this one 'The Delusion of Lasting Success'.

Charles Sinclair, Chairman of Associated British Foods, warns: 'Don't be late in responding to structural change otherwise your assets will devalue rapidly.' As Anthony Hucker, President of Giant Food, says, 'The eight most worrying words are: "Because we have always done it this way"'.

One of the more notable and public examples of this is Eastman Kodak. A pioneer in the photographic film market, Kodak dominated the market until relatively recently – in 1976 it held a 90% share of photographic film and, gallingly, Kodak actually pioneered digital photography technology in the mid-1990s but actively chose not to pursue this line of innovation because of the threat it posed to the core photographic film business.

Subsequently, other players developed the digital market (Sony, Canon, etc.), with uptake of digital leading to a commensurate decline in sales of photographic film. After initially failing to respond to the shift to digital, Kodak attempted a turnaround based on digital photography and digital printing, while also attempting to generate revenues through patent enforcement; it held a limited 7% share (7th position) of the market in 2007.

Nevertheless, Kodak clearly failed to 'convert' its brand capital in film to digital. In contrast, Fujifilm have successfully gained a foothold in digital while diversifying the business more broadly, for example into cosmetics. Kodak has failed to turn a profit since 2007, and in February 2012 filed for bankruptcy. A sad end to a masterful brand.

Kodak failed to follow one of the basic rules of strategy: if you are going to be cannibalized then it is, on balance, better to cannibalize yourself!

5 Failure to employ the best possible team

Putting up with a sub-par or mediocre team will make your strategy unachievable or sub-optimized at best. To illustrate this we will add the word 'bureaucracy' to the word 'mediocracy'. It's a problem with which most CEOs are all too familiar. 'You can never kill middle-management bureaucracy,' Peter Lau, CEO of Giordano International, notes wryly. 'It always grows back.'

In the case of Microsoft, bureaucracy and mediocracy went hand-in-hand. Microsoft remains one of the world's foremost technology and software companies; however, over recent years it has seen the step change improvement of its competitor, Apple, to a position where a single Apple product, the iPhone, generates more revenues than all of Microsoft's products combined. What went wrong?

While Microsoft has continued to generate products that are successful, it has not been the source of stellar innovations – it is argued that Microsoft's structures for internal talent management effectively crippled its ability to innovate by promoting internal competition, within teams, at the expense of competing in the wider market.

By employing a management system known as 'stack ranking', in which each unit is forced to declare a certain percentage of employees as top performers, good performers, average and poor, Microsoft created tension and competition among its most valuable resource – the innovators.

In a recent feature on the company in *Vanity Fair*, journalist Kurt Eichenwald reported, 'Every current and former Microsoft employee I interviewed – every one – cited stack ranking as the most destructive process inside of Microsoft, something that drove out untold numbers of employees.' Eichenwald quotes a former software developer saying, 'If you were on a team of ten people, you walked in the first day knowing that, no matter how good everyone was, two people were going to get a great review, seven were going to get mediocre reviews, and one was going to get a terrible review.'

Ed McCahill, who worked at Microsoft as a marketing manager for 16 years, says, 'You look at the Windows Phone and you can't help but wonder – how did Microsoft squander the lead they had with the Windows CE devices? They had a great lead, they were years ahead. And they completely blew it. And they completely blew it because of the bureaucracy.'[2]

The cumulative effect of the system within Microsoft appears to have been twofold – stifling potentially successful innovations (e.g. an early prototype e-reader) and causing an exodus of talent who did not want to be part of a crushing, bureaucratic system. Microsoft bizarrely achieved mediocracy by apparently introducing a system designed to do the opposite – identify and reward the best.

A bad case of 'unintended consequences'.

6 Failure to focus

However seductive proliferation and diversification are, a failure to 'stick to the strategic knitting' will take you off course.

Take the example of Adidas. Following a change of ownership after the founder Adolf Dassler's family sold the company in 1987, Adidas added a range of brands (e.g. Pony, Le Coq Sportif) and various product lines including clothing, perfume and accessories to their core footwear offering. This did not work!

Losses totalled $100m in 1992, with sales 25% lower than a decade earlier at $1.5bn. In 1993, Robert Louis-Dreyfus and Christian Tourres took control of the business and returned it to growth by shifting focus back to core sportswear and disposing of brands that did not fit the category. By 1995 Adidas was generating $163m profit on $3.4bn sales. In 2009 sales hit nearly $15bn.

And if that is not convincing enough then take the example of General Motors. GM is the largest global car manufacturer by vehicle sales units (2011). Yet despite the apparent scale advantage, GM has struggled to perform in recent years. Pundits put this down almost entirely to the company's loss of market focus.

GM boasted a complex portfolio of 'divisions, brands within divisions, models within brands'. To the consumer, this did not translate into more choice. It translated into massive confusion – GM's website listed more than 95 cars in 2009. To add insult to injury, GM continued to launch new vehicles (19 in 2009) while not decommissioning older models at a similar rate.

The end result of this was a highly fragmented and inefficient corporate overhead and manufacturing base combined with a glut of choice for consumers. The economic downturn exacerbated these pressures and GM filed for bankruptcy in 2009, following which its brand portfolio was extensively restructured – the Pontiac, Saturn, Hummer and other brands being laid to rest – leaving GM with four core brands (Chevrolet, Cadillac, GMC and Buick). While the long-term outlook is unsure, at least there is hope that a focused portfolio will allow management to concentrate on what is really important.

The key to avoiding this pitfall is to learn to say 'NO'. 'NO' to diversification for its own sake, 'NO' to unwarranted proliferation of product range, 'NO' to unnecessary geographical expansion, and so on.

7 Inability to foster belief in the strategy

If the leadership does not communicate the strategy consistently and with passion then the rest of the company will not 'believe'. Corporate memories for strategy announcements are short. But memories of a failure are very long. Combined with a lack of focus on measures/outcomes/quick wins, a failure to continually and consistently reinforce the strategy will undermine it, and belief in it will wane. Communication of the strategy in the right way to the critical stakeholder groups is critical – keeping it simple but convincing pays dividends. Getting people to buy into it makes it easier to implement and to implement well.

The history of Mercedes' efforts to build a sub-compact car for city driving illustrates this point. It took Mercedes engineers 10–15 years to embrace the concept of designing a small car, despite the fact that it was clearly an important element in Mercedes' strategy. The company as a whole did not 'believe' with sufficient fervour and, as a result, what began in the late 1970s and early 1980s as a visionary design effort took nearly two decades to come to fruition, with the first Smart launching as late as 1997.[3]

8 Inability to translate the strategy into a corporate 'purpose'

Increasingly enterprises need an enduring purpose to inspire, engage and motivate their people. The whole team needs to know that what they are doing matters to the company … and increasingly to society. Walmart got there first with its promise to get low-priced goods to everyone in a community-friendly way.

As the profit motive alone is devalued as an unintended consequence of the 2008–2012 recession; the absence of a 'purpose' will diminish the effectiveness of the strategy.

Sony might be a modern day example of how a well-intentioned management inadvertently 'ripped the heart out' of the corporate culture of an otherwise very successful firm. Sony's co-founder, Akio Morita, was known as relatively 'un-Japanese' in his leadership of the company – emphasizing innovation and new products and markets as the core focus of the company, while supporting this with strong industrial strategies to achieve low cost and thus making products highly competitive.

His successors, in particular Sir Howard Stringer, apparently eschewed this innovation focus in favour of a strongly industrial 'MBA style' leadership focused primarily on driving the business through volume growth and cost reduction. Sony, therefore, focused on a narrow product set to increase volume, developing a culture that increasingly centred on cost-cutting and gave less and less emphasis to innovation and developing new products and markets.

The loss of charismatic purpose and leadership from Sony has not only meant that it has lost out in key battles over recent years – e-readers, electronic music, televisions – but has also led to a fall of confidence among investors that Sony has the capability to resurrect its market leadership. The uphill task that now confronts Sony's new CEO, Kazuo Hirai, cannot be overestimated.

As A. Vellayan, Executive Chairman of India's Murugappa Group, observes: 'Strategy should allow us to create a positive impact on the ecosystem of each of our businesses (on vendors, customers, suppliers, employees, regulators, society in general). This is the best way to become sustainable and have a purpose beyond just making money.'

9 Failure to instil a sense of pace

'If you are slow, you are behind,' notes Jan Michiel Hessels, Chairman of NYSE Euronext. There are countless examples of companies lulling themselves into a sense of security about the speed at which they have to move. There is little upside, if any, in delaying once you are convinced that a certain reality is true, whether it is positive or negative. For instance, in terms of bad news, then it is usually the case that the sooner you announce it, the better. Act earlier – bad news does not improve with age. To quote Eric Kintz, Senior Vice-President and General Manager of Logitech for Business: 'Strategy now becomes a framework rather than a detailed plan. Historically you did a three-year strategy plan, a two-year product plan and a one-year budget. Now that things are moving so fast, you need to set a three-year strategic framework, a one-year product and financial plan and then everything needs to be worked on in a quarterly process. Anything more rigid than this risks being out of touch with the market.'

'If you are slow, you are behind.'

And if it relates to an investment or some market entry priority, then if you do not act rapidly, there is a danger that one of your competitors might get there first in terms of signing up a key supplier, a key distributor, acquiring the critical partner for entry into a new geography, and the like. Sitting on your hands while the world changes is never going to be a winning strategy.

A classic example of when not just a company, but an entire industry, failed to adapt to changing times is that of the music industry. In the early days of MP3 files, different strands of the music industry were united in their denial of the take-up of this new technology. Key players in the industry convinced themselves that CDs were, despite appearances, here to stay, and that so long as file-sharing resources, such as Napster, were fought in the courts, the fundamental economics of the industry would not change. The result, as everyone knows, is Apple's history.

Apple saw, and indeed drove, the changing economics and, with the launch and rise of iTunes, iPods, etc., came to dominate the industry, sucking revenue from record companies previously sitting pretty on fat profits. The record companies failed to see the need to enable monetization from the new technology and merely tried to prevent it being used without payment.

It took Apple to create software and products that enabled profit, and it was Apple that gained substantially from this monetization, not the companies who made the music.

10 Failure to create accountability for results

The heart and soul of execution is accountability – it is this that motivates people to follow through on their commitments. It is essential with any plan that it is clear who is responsible for what, and it is vital for the business that accountability is tied to results, not activities. Steps that lead clearly towards finish lines are needed to ensure that individuals and teams are accountable for progress towards strategic objectives. This is essential because, while activity within an organization is unceasing, it is only results that really matter. Highly rewarding those who have achieved results is another vital part of the process. As Barry Judge, CEO of LivingSocial, says: 'Everything in management is about accountability and strategy is no different. Any strategy which does not identify metrics and accountability is flawed.' Carlos Medeiros, CEO of BRMALLS, advises: 'The appraisal system needs to mirror the strategy and, for simplicity's sake, have everyone focused on the five most important things they can do to execute the strategy and keep them accountable for them.'

The rise and subsequent dramatic fall of Enron International was due to many things: overweening hubris among people who were sure that they were the 'smartest guys in the room'; lax regulatory oversight; and, not least, a massive failure of accountability. It is well documented that Enron lurched into crisis due to the uncovering of systematic, institutional fraud whereby profits were recorded for planned constructions that hadn't yet yielded any profit; indeed, profits were recorded for deals that subsequently fell through. As the company rotted from the inside out, staff were rewarded with bonuses based on the projected profits the deals were due to make. When no such profits emerged, there was no one to be held accountable for this: the people who had struck the deal had banked their bonuses and moved on to different projects or even companies.

Fortune reporters Bethany McLean and Peter Elkind, who wrote extensively on Enron, concluded that the corporate culture that Enron's bosses Jeffrey Skilling and Andrew Fastow and others had built up made financial deception almost inevitable. Staff were encouraged to play by their own rules: there was no foundation of a system of accountability whereby people were rewarded for actual results achieved, or held responsible when things went wrong.

* * *

There must be other reasons why strategy fails but, having shared these with most of our CEO interviewees, we are reasonably confident that these ten pitfalls cover the vast majority of them.

Excessive short-termism is the first, which Marks & Spencer fell prey to in the late 1990s in a bid to be the first UK retailer to achieve £1bn annual profits. To avoid this pitfall it is vital to manage the trade-off between long-term objectives and short-term expectations. Ignoring external trends, particularly challenging ones, is another clear pitfall and one which tripped up RIM, makers of the one-time groundbreaking BlackBerry devices. They failed to change as the market around them changed and the rest is Apple's history. Overconfidence based upon existing success is a third pitfall, where the continuing attraction of a business model to a company's existing customers creates blinkers to the underlying problem: lack of interest by future customers. The recent demise of Blockbuster is a classic example. Many companies in recent years have fallen into the fourth pitfall: failure to respond to structural changes in the market. Take the example of Kodak who continued to cling to their film business and only attempted a major switch to digital when it was too late. Another giant company, Microsoft, exemplifies the fifth pitfall, failing to motivate and reward the best people. Microsoft's stack ranking method of performance and reward was a behemoth system that created unnecessary tension and competition in the company's most valuable resource: the innovators.

Our sixth pitfall, that of failure to focus, is again one that many recent companies have fallen into, Adidas being a prime example. In the 1980s Adidas added numerous brands and product lines which clouded the company focus, and where falling focus led, falling profits followed. New management turned around the company, by shifting it back to a core focus on sportswear, and returned it to profitability. Fighting disbelief in the strategy is another vital element of strategy execution, which Mercedes signally failed to achieve – it took the company nearly 20 years to bring to fruition the strategy of launching a compact city car because of opposition to the strategy from many elements inside the company. Sony may be an example of a company that was unable to translate strategy into corporate 'purpose', the eighth pitfall, when new management fostered a culture increasingly centred on cost-cutting rather than innovation. The subsidence of not just individual music companies, but the entire music industry itself, is a clear example of the ninth pitfall: failing to keep up with the pace of change. By clinging to the CD as a distribution method and failing to adapt to technological developments, the music industry's demise mirrored Apple's rise. The catastrophic collapse and very public humiliation of Enron and its employees is about as clear an example as there can be for our final pitfall, the failure to create accountability for results.

If you avoid these ten pitfalls, you are well on the way to executing your strategy effectively.

. . . and ten ways to get it right

'The blindingly obvious usually trips you up.' PETER SWINBURN, PRESIDENT AND CEO, MOLSON COORS

Across our partner and CEO interviews, the list of admired companies was not as long as we had expected. Enduring success is more elusive than one would have imagined. In fact, there were only three that seemed to come through frequently as top of the list for avoiding many if not all of the ten deadly sins outlined in the previous chapter: IBM, Apple (of course) and Amazon.

IBM because of its ability to change strategy (at least twice in its past 40 years) and still remain a powerful and successful company.

Apple because of its ability to identify consumer needs before consumers know them themselves.

Amazon for its relentless pursuit of a strategy of online ordering and home delivery capability that only now is beginning to scare practically every retailer in the world.

Instead of falling prey to the deadly sins, these companies succeeded in:

Creating bold strategies that had real, tangible and demonstrable customer/consumer value as well as competitive distinctiveness and corporate purpose.

Hiring the best people to implement them and communicating to them clearly the future strategy and what their role involved.

Pursuing a focused strategy in a consistent, single-minded way.

Adapting rapidly wherever necessary by closely scrutinizing developing market trends.

In short, they avoided some if not all of the 'blindingly obvious' things that trip you up, and that Peter Swinburn, CEO of Molson Coors, warns against.

Rather than hoping for the nirvana of avoiding all ten sins, let's just look at examples of avoiding each one in turn. Rather than review them as pitfalls, we will now examine their mirror-images – virtues!

- Long-termism
- Being in tune with the market
- Humility
- Moving to the next business model early
- Meritocracy
- Focus
- Consistency
- Purpose
- Pace
- Accountability

1 Long-termism

Amazon has proved itself to be a formidable strategic player in the online field. The vision for the company was set by Jeff Bezos two decades ago and he still believes it. Increasingly, so do his competitors and investors.

When the company went public in 1997, Bezos was clear about his strategy: 'It's all about the long term,' he said, warning shareholders that decision-making processes in Amazon might be different than in other companies, and urging potential investors to ensure Amazon's long-term approach fitted within their investment policy.

And he was not joking. Amazon has been known often to prioritize long-term investment over short-term margins and dividend payouts, in order to improve business resilience. In a 2011 shareholder meeting, Bezos articulated his manifesto clearly: 'If you invent frequently and are willing to fail, then you never get to that point where you really need to bet the whole company … we are going to continue to plant seeds. And I can guarantee you that not everything we do will work.'

Amazon's strategy was evident with the launch of Amazon's Kindle and Kindle Fire, which were viewed by Bezos as a service rather than a product – a means to an end. He was willing to sell Amazon's core tablet at a loss of about a quarter of its retail price, seeing it as a valuable point of sale to Amazon's virtual marketplace. Despite making a loss in the short term, this strategy seems to be working – analysts estimate that each tablet sold is generating Amazon more than $130 in additional revenue throughout its three-year lifetime, generating an operating margin of more than 20%.

Bezos' vision is paying off – Amazon's stock has soared by over 12,000% since its initial public offering, and its long-term prospects appear positive. Indeed, it is difficult to find a retail CEO today who does not mention Amazon as their (potentially) biggest competitor.

Of equal note must be the raft of smaller highly successful private companies who quietly manage to transform themselves outside the public gaze. Indeed, we would argue that this is the core strength of the German Mittelstand companies – small, often family-owned companies producing high-quality products in a consistent and predictable way.

Finally, we would rank the private equity industry as scoring high on long-termism. Many people describe the PE industry as short-termist, but OC&C thinks that this characterization is an oversimplification. At the end of the day, PE firms only make money if they can sell the business to either the public markets or another buyer. Either way, they are unlikely to be able to sell an empty shell.

They have to create a vibrant business – albeit one that is preoccupied with performance – which has a long-term future, or the PE model does not work. And it does. PE firms do all the heavy lifting in terms of transformation behind the closed doors of private ownership so that the business can emerge into public view four to eight years later. However much value they create for themselves, they still leave plenty for the next owner to enjoy!

2 Being in tune with the market

Google uses its staff very effectively to be the eyes and ears of the organization, asking them to think like customers one day a week and even asking its own technologists to attack it from time to time to see how its systems respond. 'Big companies can fall into the trap of worrying about the needs of the bosses rather than the needs of the customers,' notes Andy Harrison, CEO of Whitbread. Google is careful to avoid this temptation.

Zara, the fashion retailer owned by Inditex, is another business that's precisely in tune with its market. Zara's ability to divine changes in taste among its clientele and then to satisfy them in a matter of weeks is legendary. Its supply chain is designed specifically to cope with this 'rapid response' requirement. Zara continuously tracks market trends and customer preferences, monitoring store sales as well as the media, and employing trend-spotters who target venues such as university campuses and nightclubs.

Zara's supply chain response to its field coverage is very quick – when a trend is identified, a design can be converted into garments in less than two weeks, with the capability of having it in store within four to five weeks. The traditional industry model takes up to six months. Zara, therefore, has a significant competitive advantage and stays well ahead of its market.

3 Humility

For years, one heard a great deal about Walmart and Target in terms of leading US retailers, but working quietly in the background was Walgreens.

Walgreens is a first-class beauty and health convenience format with a 14% share of the US health and beauty market, just getting on with the job and delivering value to customers and investors through growth and profits. Its recently announced merger with Boots would appear to be a ringing endorsement of its coming of age.

Historically, Walgreens' biggest strength has been its knowledge of its customers. By understanding that customers prioritize convenience, Walgreens implemented a saturation-style store expansion plan, knowing that proximity to a Walgreens is an important factor in retaining customers. In 2012, more than three-quarters of the US population live within five miles of a Walgreens.

Product mix diversification was another way that Walgreens boosted its footfall, increasingly offering services such as blood tests at hundreds of locations. The company is also focusing on its multichannel offering, with the purchase of Drugstore.com for more than $400m substantially increasing its online presence. In addition to focusing on customer care, Walgreens has invested attention and resource to develop its employee base, and has steadily managed to decrease churn rate. And all of this has been done outside the glare of the PR spotlight.

Indeed, Walgreens' impressive growth has historically been characterized by a sense of humility. Despite being a very creative retailer, pioneering products such as the malted milkshake and services such as multilingual prescriptions and drive-thru pharmacies, the company never went out of its way to seek excessive credit for its innovations.

It is this humble state of mind that has helped to make Walgreens a sound investment prospect, and an incredibly capable and consistent retailer for more than a century. 2011 was Walgreens' 37th consecutive year of record sales despite a challenging economy, and its stock price has risen by over 500% since 1995. Walgreens' shareholders have been paid dividends for over 300 consecutive quarters, with the board increasing the dividend rate annually. With its 2012 purchase of a 45% stake in UK-based Alliance Boots, Walgreens is now part of the world's largest pharmacy chain.

4 Moving to the next business model early

This is the classic 'innovators' dilemma'. When you have something new do you cannibalize yourself – or put the disruptive model in a bottom drawer hoping that no one will ever come across it?

As we have seen the classic strategists' answer is to cannibalize yourself and get on with it in a measured but inexorable way.

Generally speaking if you do not do it to yourself then someone will definitely do it to you eventually and often in a very painful and humiliating fashion, as Kodak found out the hard way. The manufacturers of televisions, on the other hand, have been exemplary in terms of being prepared to cannibalize themselves. They have seamlessly moved from plasma to LCD to LED and added HD and 3D on the way through. It does not seem to have occurred to them to stop and try to milk the very significant investments that had been made in the previous technology.

'Be willing to adapt if the situation requires it.'

'Sticking to "old beliefs" can be life-threatening,' emphasizes Nancy McKinstry, CEO of Wolters Kluwer. 'Be willing to adapt if the situation requires it.'

Another example of a business responding fast to market changes and making a decision to cannibalize itself early on is one of the UK's leading daily newspapers, the *Daily Mail*. The *Mail* was quick to respond to the decline in circulation of print media, and launched its internationally appealing *Mail Online* website. The website is a prime source of news for the masses – focusing on the sensational, scandals and showbiz, creating a very 'clickable' offering easily translated across countries.

The *Mail Online* is now the most-read newspaper website in the world, having overtaken *The New York Times*. In 2012, it has approximately 100 million unique visitors per month, who access the website from more than 200 countries. What is even more impressive is that the British site is ranked fourth by US readers among US newspaper websites.

Almost a quarter of its visits originate from mobile devices, and its readership is younger and more affluent than average internet users, making it prime advertising space. In fact, the *Mail* believes it is now a different calibre from other newspaper websites, and insists that its webpage should be compared to web giants such as MSN and AOL ... and it is probably right.

DMGT, owner of the newspaper, took a calculated risk with its ambitious launch of the *Mail Online* website, and had to endure losses for several years following an investment of £25m. However, its patience has paid off, and the website has been profitable since summer 2012.

As we saw in Chapter 7, General Motors was forced to file for bankruptcy in 2009. The company subsequently launched a reorganization that involved the sale or closure of brands including Hummer, Oldsmobile, Pontiac, Saab and Saturn. For GM, these changes were a matter of life or death. In contrast, Ford did something similar, but much earlier.

In 2006, the company embarked on a vast restructuring effort that involved halting production of unprofitable models and the closure of 14 factories. Across the company, brand silos were disbanded, as the company closed or sold off a selection of marques including Jaguar Cars, Land Rover, Aston Martin and Mercury. Ford also sold off a 20% holding in Mazda, surrendering control of the company.

These reorganizations were root-and-branch affairs that reflected decades of market share decline. However, because Ford took action early, it was able to retain its independence at the height of the financial crisis. GM, by contrast, was forced to seek Chapter 11 bankruptcy protection and accept government bail-out funding of up to $50bn.

The moral of these stories is to move early, however painful it might be. Shareholders will not thank you for dallying along the way and frittering away their money.

5 Meritocracy

In terms of consistently going after the best people and then motivating them to do extraordinary things, one has to immediately cite Goldman Sachs. A corporate culture that rewards top performers and terminates bottom performers could perhaps appear somewhat ruthless, but it remains a successful one for this leading global investment bank, in which demand for jobs continues strong. Goldman Sachs Chairman and CEO Lloyd Blankfein disclosed that almost 300,000 individuals applied for a full-time position at Goldman Sachs in 2010 and 2011, with fewer than 4% getting jobs.

Even though there are from time to time 'dissenters' who question the merits of this model (sometimes very vocally – viz. the recent farewell speech by an executive director about exploitation of clients and indifference to staff), Goldman Sachs has nevertheless consistently recruited the highest performers and turned them into the most committed professionals in the field. They have also communicated this to the world and there is widespread belief in the company's performance standards, meaning that people are therefore appropriately either impressed (clients) or scared (competitors).

A more mainstream example, Nordstrom, the US department store, can be applauded for achieving outstanding levels of staff commitment and customer satisfaction – pretty important in the retail world.

The retailer constantly articulates to its employees that they are there for the long-haul, and are expected to perform in line with the company's high expectations. Most managers are promoted from within after proving themselves and moving up the ranks, and practically everyone has shop-floor experience, sending a message that all employees are valued and everyone can succeed.

Decentralized buying empowers store employees and creates unique store offerings, while demonstrating a level of trust in regional managers and individual store operators. Nordstrom's emphasis on retailing and workforce excellence signals to employees that they have a job worth keeping and in which they can make great progress.

The company is famous for its employee handbook, a single card with 75 words emphasizing the importance of good customer relations, and asking employees to simply use their best judgement in any situation. In recent years the card has been accompanied by a more comprehensive booklet with rules and regulations, but the myth is here to stay.

A more 21st-century example is the much vilified private equity industry. Despite their early reputation – well-earned in some cases – for being preoccupied with financial leverage and with creating shareholder value (often for themselves), there is no doubt that they are very clinical about their investment thesis (their winning business model) and the team that they think they need to deliver it. They bring new management in early and with little hesitation – they want to optimize their chances of success and believe that having the right managers is the way to do it. We agree.

6 Focus

If you want precision engineering and performance driving at an almost affordable price then you buy a Porsche ... and most likely a Porsche 911, which is still around after many decades.

The Porsche brand has been synonymous with sports cars since its early days. But in order to increase its reach in the car market, the company has diversified in recent years to produce more practical models and appeal to a larger customer base. The diversification has proved to be successful, with Porsche's Cayenne model, a family-friendly crossover, now generating a larger chunk of Porsche's profit than the 911, and accounting for 45% of Porsche's total sales volume in the United States.

However, Porsche is making an effort not to overstretch the brand and to keep it in line with its sporty image, an image that allows Porsche to achieve some of the healthiest profit margins in the industry. Porsche's CEO, Matthias Müller, identifies the importance of this heritage, and describes a strategy in which, whenever a model is released that is not directly a sports car, a new sports car model has to be launched simultaneously to maintain the brand image. Indeed, Porsche provides a fine example for the importance of focus for a successful brand, even when its product range is expanding.

Similarly, IKEA has proven itself to be a prime example of an iconic and focused business, endeavouring to stay close to its initial aims. IKEA's products have a unique identity, while still having the capability of meeting many different client needs.

The company offers a wide range of good value-for-money products in a very focused market sector. IKEA has a very clear focus on furniture and furnishings and its products emphasize function, design and good value. This has resulted in near universal success, with Ikea being a strong player in all the markets in which it is active. An impressive achievement by any standard.

7 Consistency

Warren Buffett has made a virtue of consistency. His consistent mantra about investing in real businesses, that do real things for real people and where cash flow counts, is difficult to fault. And shareholders agree.

Consistency is a preventative measure against exposure to risk, as it significantly reduces uncertainty. The core of Warren Buffett's investing philosophy is simple: a consistent track record is likely to result in consistent share price growth. Sharp gains and volatility, as well as reliance on passing trends, are unpredictable and risky.

Berkshire Hathaway Share Price development

Source: OC&C Strategy Consultants

Buffett clearly knows a thing or two about investing – Berkshire Hathaway, the conglomerate he chairs, has been averaging an annual growth in book value of over 20% for more than four decades, producing high returns when the S&P 500 was making a loss, making it one of the largest public companies in the world.

8 Purpose

How do you get the employees to 'buy in' to the proposition and yet not have to 'buy' their loyalty with high pay and expensive benefits?

Both Gap and Starbucks cracked this problem and made their missions so important – and even cool – that for long periods of time they had people flocking to their doors to work with them even though the jobs were essentially straightforward retail jobs. Bringing good coffee and the American preppy fashion style to the American nation was made to be 'cool'.

Starbucks and Gap proved that with innovative store designs, and by hiring young, engaging people, working in retail could become extremely fashionable, despite the fact that the actual work differed very little from that in other companies. Both chains make an effort publicly to treat their employees with respect – Gap operates employee-only shopping events, and rewards outstanding staff with five-figure bonuses, while Starbucks refers to all its employees as 'partners'. This is a much cheaper strategy than paying workers above-market wages, and it appears to be just as useful in pleasing employees and positioning a brand as a good place to work.

Career progression from sales associate or barista to store and regional manager is emphasized, creating a sense of a great career opportunity rather than a temporary retail job. Additionally, emphasizing links to the community as well as ethical sourcing improves the brands' images, and makes them appear to be positive places to work. Indeed, these factors, as well as rewarding employees with a bag of coffee a week or a 30% staff discount, prove to be more than enough to create sought-after retail jobs.

Instilling this sense of purpose has an enormous commercial benefit – the enthusiasm and service ethos of the staff is infectious. And so we all went into Starbucks and Gap and spent a ton of money on coffee (three to five times what you normally would expect to spend on a cup of coffee) and white tee shirts (for sale at up to twice the price of those in other mainstream suppliers). The staff had drunk the Kool-Aid – and we drank it next!

9 Pace

Amazon is a classic success story of a company that saw the potential of a new model, moved quickly to build up market share and established an overwhelmingly dominant market position that has proved unassailable. Amazon's success sprang partly from being first to spot a regulatory loophole and exploit it – namely, the US Supreme Court ruling that companies without physical presences need not pay sales taxes. It also sprang partly from being first to market with a patented product with their ownership of 'one-click' purchasing.

Above all, success has come from the fact that Amazon was the first to establish trust in a mass model at a time when online shopping was just beginning, and then building on this to create market dominance. As Jeff Bezos has said: 'Market leadership can translate directly to higher revenue, higher profitability, greater capital velocity, and correspondingly stronger returns on invested capital.'

Amazon has retained its market position by constantly innovating, for example with the launch of the Kindle, and by putting the customer at the centre of its operations. Almost no one is keeping up the breathtaking pace that Amazon is setting in the online retail world.

10 Accountability

In a small company it is often easy to identify who is responsible for what, and how they should be rewarded if they succeed. This is much harder in large organizations, but no less vital. Virgin, however, appears to have cracked it, despite being a vast multinational company. They have erected systems for accountability and reward at the heart of the organization.

Virgin's staff bonus scheme not only rewards top managers, but is designed also to incentivize staff at all levels of the organization, whether they be frontline customer-facing staff or in back-office supporting roles. As Virgin moves into more and more areas of business, it retains this focus on the need for clear accountability – and the potential benefits thereof for those who perform well.

Another example of an organization that prioritizes accountability is the Swedish bank Handelsbanken. This bank operates very differently from most of its competitors and claims to have weathered the recent financial storms correspondingly much better. Indeed, during the Swedish banking crisis of the 1990s, Handelsbanken was the only bank not to seek a governmental bailout.

Handelsbanken's model is one of major decentralization: branch managers are fully responsible for all business transactions with their customers, whether individual or corporate and regardless of size. For any credit to be granted it has to be approved at branch level. Indeed the accountability goes deeper than this: loans that staff members grant stay with them for the lifetime of the loan, so that at any time it is plain to see who made which loans and whether their decisions were good or poor.

The reward system for employees is equally unconventional: Handelsbanken does not give bonuses. 'Handelsbanken believes bonuses should be avoided in risk-taking operations, mainly because they risk providing the wrong incentives. Consequently, the bank has no bonus programme for any members of management or for any staff in the branch office operations, who all work on flat salaries.' Salaries are determined according to performance targets, and instead of bonus rewards the bank operates a profit-sharing system, the Oktogonen, whereby all staff are rewarded, at retirement age, according to the historic profits of the overall bank. Employees' rewards are based on length of service only; position and salary are not taken into account.

The bank's accountability and reward systems have proved very effective. Handelsbanken consistently records higher profitability than all its closest competitors and is moving from strength to strength. In 2007, it had 50 branches in the UK; five years later it has more than doubled that number.

* * *

So avoiding the pitfalls and turning vices into virtues can be done. None of us, therefore, has an excuse for not going down the 'righteous path of strategy development and execution'.

In this chapter, we have seen how companies have avoided our ten deadly strategy pitfalls and turned vices into virtues. Amazon is a shining example of a company and its leader taking the long view and keeping up with the pace of change. Zara is a retailer that has consistently kept in tune with the market and has growing profits and a global footprint to prove it. The American retailer that has kept below the radar, Walgreens, provides an object lesson in humility and success through all-embracing knowledge of its customers. The *Daily Mail*'s hard-fought ownership of a portion of cyber space profits, with the *Mail Online* finally entering the black in the summer of 2012, is a good example of a company that moved to a new business model early.

Goldman Sachs, for all of its critics, is an object lesson in meritocracy in a company; through the years it has recruited the highest performers and turned them into the most committed professionals. IKEA's relentless strength in furniture and furnishings has us holding them up as a beacon for corporate focus, and Warren Buffett's constant insistence on investing in real businesses that do real things for real people is a model of consistency. Gap and Starbucks are two companies that instil a sense of purpose in their employees: both companies have clear paths of career progression and emphasize links with the community. Starbucks refers to all employees as 'partners', and Gap creates happenings such as employee only shopping events. Lastly, we find that the accountability of Virgin's staff bonus scheme incentivizes staff at all levels and is an excellent model of good accountability enabling the driving forward of strategy.

We need to remember the sins and the virtues and take a good look at how we are shaping up on a regular basis. And if we shape up well, then the markets and stakeholders will reward the company and their clearly visionary leadership!

9

Tips for new leaders

'Ask all the dumb questions. Because you can.' DOUG IVESTER, FORMER CHAIRMAN AND CEO, THE COCA-COLA COMPANY

By now we have talked about strategy development, execution, how to fail and how to succeed. To finish, we wanted to err on the side of the practical.

As a new CEO, how do you get to grips with your company, which may or may not be perfectly formed strategically? As consultants often do, we thought of creating a checklist of things that an incoming leader should do. Then we thought again.

We decided it would be much better to rely on our CEO interviewees to provide a guide to what a new recruit to that august group should focus on. Our CEO colleagues excelled themselves and consistently homed in on a few very high value tips for the newcomers in their midst. While many were rather sceptical about the good old 'CEO's First 100 Days' representing the be-all-and-end-all of what the CEO should be doing about strategy, they had some very sound alternatives.

Meet the people

The most telling advice was:

> *Walk the corridors and meet the frontline people*

'When you go into a new company as a CEO, most people have no clue what they are getting into,' says Dean Finch, Group Chief Executive of National Express. 'Talk to as many people as you can to find out what is really going on – the frontline people, not just the managers.'

With the best will in the world, your immediate team will not be able to give you the real picture. Instead, you should 'talk to people who have less of a vested interest – your employees as well as stakeholders, advisors, consultants, and so on,' suggests Paul Manduca, Chairman of Prudential.

You need to talk to as many of the true frontline workers as possible and try radical ways of gaining insight into just how good your company is. For example, phone your company's helplines to see how customer-centric your new organization really is.

Jerry Fowden, CEO of Cott Corporation, suggests: 'Use your first two to three months to visit your factories, customers, debt and equity holders and even the canteen. You'll never have the opportunity again and it's important to understand what is going on across the whole business and to start to get people "on side".'

Until the new CEO has formed his or her own view about what is going on, the inbuilt filters that senior management naturally apply to all of the information flowing up inside organizations need to be put to one side. You need to discover whether the current business model is working or not. Charles Sinclair, Chairman of Associated British Foods, agrees: 'Most companies don't tap the extraordinary amount of valuable information in their junior people. Especially those who deal with customers.'

Talk to the stakeholders

Understanding the perspective of stakeholders – and, if possible, gaining their trust at an early stage – will be a valuable asset. This will pay dividends later, when you have to take them along the strategic journey with you. 'We invest a great deal of time in structured dialogue with our shareholders,' says Alexis Duval,

President of Tereos. 'As a result, decisions don't come as a surprise to them, and we're better positioned to make quick decisions when necessary.'

Arno Mahlert, former CEO and CFO of maxingvest, suggests that you can use the information you gather to improve the business. 'Talk to a lot of people: employees, customers, suppliers, even competitors or people who know your competitors. Then act on any identified weaknesses, any blind spots that affect the way your company sees the market.'

Work out the fundamental business model of the current business

Most businesses at their core are very simple. The number of things that you need to get right is relatively small. Understanding the two or three things that will make the difference between success and failure will short-circuit a number of steps in the strategy process. It will also give you an early steer as to whether the business is sustainable, whether the essential factor for success is low cost, superior customer service, intellectual property or something else. Whatever it is, you need to identify it and come to a view as to whether it is robust enough to endure.

'Know the mechanics of your industry.'

Cees 't Hart, CEO of FrieslandCampina, is certain that this is a critical element in the armoury of the new CEO. 'You have to understand the dominant logic of your company,' he says. 'You need to challenge that logic, to find out whether it is still valid and applicable.' Dr Kurt-Ludwig Gutberlet, Chairman and CEO of Bosch and Siemens Home Appliances, concurs. 'You need to know the mechanics of your industry. A surprising number of companies behave in ways that show that they don't understand the fundamental logic of their industry.'

Think radically about the business

'You always have to ask yourself whether conventional wisdom is right,' says Graham Mckay, Chairman of SABMiller. 'Often it is not!'

Even if you ultimately confirm that the current business model is great and no change is necessary, at least you will have tested it to destruction. At this point, you can be confident that it is robust.

'You need to find the sustainable differentiation and then understand how far it can take you,' says Claus-Dietrich Lahrs, CEO of Hugo Boss. 'Without this, you are lost.'

Assess your people rigorously

We have argued earlier that having the right people in the right roles will make or break your strategy. So draw your co-conspirators close and check that they truly believe and are not just paying lip-service. Check the quality of your team beyond the conspirators, too. The sooner you make people-related changes, the better.

Penny Hughes, a serial Non-Executive Director, advises, 'Review the team early, be single-minded about what you need, get it right.' It's a lot less painful this way, too. 'Get to know the top 75 and assess them well,' advises John Brock, Chairman and CEO of Coca-Cola Enterprises. 'Intuitive judgement is fine. You will almost always be right.'

Where you need to, don't be reluctant taking in new blood and giving them the backing they need. 'New guys almost always change the team,' says James Lawrence, Chairman of Rothschilds North America. 'They need to get the right support and capabilities.'

Guilherme Loureiro, former Head of Corporate Strategy at Unilever, Brazil, advises 'Managers who cannot – or do not wish to – align with strategy need to leave.'

Trust your judgement

'Our strategy definition process is extremely basic,' says Jean-François Palus, Deputy CEO of PPR. 'We tend to rely on convictions, on key people's gut feelings.' First impressions matter. Your first impressions are probably the same as other people's.

'Don't always wait for more information, analysis, insight,' says Bert Meerstadt, CEO of NS Dutch Railways. 'Sometimes you need to follow your intuition and dare to intervene when you think it is appropriate.'

Act rapidly and decisively

If something needs fixing or someone needs to be moved (even out of the organization) there is no upside to delay. Problems generally get worse with time not better. And you are more likely to be forgiven early on in your tenure as CEO than later. Move faster, cut deeper, reorganize decisively. Remember, pace can be a competitive weapon.

'You need to accept you are making business judgements in

a fast-moving world with incomplete information,' says former Logica CEO Andy Green. 'The key things to remember are the need for nimbleness and good timing. Timescales are collapsing.'

Search for the purpose of the business

This is not the same as trying to identify the ideal strategy or business model.

What I mean by 'purpose' is this: the secret (actually not so secret) statement about the company that will motivate people, filling them with passion about the company and their role in it. As Frits van Eerd, CEO of Jumbo Supermarkten, points out, 'Building a business requires a lot of passion, a lot of pride, and a lot of fighting and hard work. I've been working non-stop for more than a decade. It's exhausting – so you have to believe in what you're doing.'

'Find out what the company believes in,' agrees John Walden, CEO of Argos. 'Simplify the story and then let people write themselves into the script.'

Be clear that you understand the culture and how it works

Depending on your objectives, the culture of the business may or may not be ideal. But you will still have to manage round it, or through it. Whether your corporate culture is an asset or liability, it is what it is. 'You have to understand the culture because it is the lens through which the organization will view strategy,' says Jim

Muehlbauer, former CFO of Best Buy. Understanding is a crucial first base to reach before any change can happen.

Focus, focus, focus

Lack of focus can suck resources away from the primary aim of the strategy. The world is full of opportunities. There is no shortage of things to do. But getting distracted from your core strategy will ultimately prove confusing (for those trying to implement the strategy) and expensive (in the sense that diluting the resources devoted to strategy implementation can only make success less likely).

Dr Rolf Kunisch, board member and former CEO of Beiersdorf, points out that 'a company shouldn't try to focus on achieving more than three to five things simultaneously. Less is more. This rule applies to strategy development, too.'

The rallying cry of the successful CEO is focus and simplicity. Rob Templeman, Chairman of Gala Coral, suggests that the successful CEO must 'galvanize the team around a few things, delivered well, at speed'. It's a sentiment shared by Claus-Dietrich Lahrs, CEO of Hugo Boss. 'Strategy becomes simpler when companies focus on their core competences and divest non-core activities,' he says. 'In this context, do not shy away from unpopular decisions.' Murilo Ferreira, CEO of Vale, echoes this sentiment: 'Simplicity and focus are mandatory for developing and executing a winning strategy.'

* * *

In summary, we have isolated a number of tips for incoming CEOs for every type of business, in every type of market. Walk the corridors and meet the frontline people, in every level and in every area, and do it early on after taking over. Talk to the stakeholders and try to understand all the different perspectives surrounding your business. Spend time working out the fundamental business model of the current business; even if you decide it needs changing, you need to know how it works now. Think radically about the business and assess the people rigorously – take nothing as a given and remember that everything is changeable, because nothing is static in the market around you. Trust your judgement and act rapidly and decisively. Search for the true purpose of the business and be clear that you understand the culture and how it works. Lastly, to carry out strategic change within this business, which may have a fully formed culture and entrenched set of purpose, you need to focus, focus, focus!

It is easy to make these sorts of checklists when you are ensconced in the warmth of your office and the comfort of your padded chair. We do not underestimate the difficulties of following these tips when your business is trying to find its way in a fast and unpredictably changing world.

On the other hand, all journeys benefit from periods of reflection and we hope that new CEOs will have a few moments to review this short list to see whether the advice of their more experienced brethren can help accelerate their careers and deliver highly valued, wealth-creating companies.

10

In summary

'As a CEO you only have two or three years to do something good; don't risk the good by trying to be perfect.' GERRY MURPHY, CHAIRMAN, THE BLACKSTONE GROUP INTERNATIONAL PARTNERS

Since the beginning of capitalist time, the formulation of strategy for a company to succeed has been vital. Much has been written on the subject of what constitutes good strategy, and tools for how to develop one, and little has changed in the past few decades in both these regards. But the context in which we develop strategy has changed beyond measure. Permanently accelerating globalization, vastly increased rate of change, entirely game-changing technological revolutions and ever-shifting regulations have created an enormously more complex world. Competitors can appear out of nowhere, companies are subject to swift and iterative feedback loops from their customer base, the amount of data and the need to process it quickly has increased dramatically. One consequence of this is that CEOs and senior management need to be more intimately involved with strategy development than ever before.

Particularly in today's ever-changing world, leaders should not be lulled by a steady bottom-line into a false sense of security. Strategy is not a zero sum game, if your position is steady state, but your competitors have a strategy for growth, then your business is going backwards in relative terms. In searching for a strategy for the future of your company you are ultimately aiming for a sense of purpose, a simple concept of what your business is for and how it can grow. Strategy is about the deployment of resources to create high and sustainable value in the company, it is not just about (short term) profit!

To commence the strategy development process, try a method called 'End-Gaming' whereby a company's leadership focuses on where they want to be, before they worry about how to get there. It's important here to think big, to have bold aims and goals that can be aspired to, rather than mediocre ones. And it's the CEO who needs to own this bold agenda. For a busy CEO running a growing business, it can be hard to make time for strategy. It is all too easy for the urgent day to day business matters to overwhelm the important but longer term issues of direction, and for strategy to be put on hold. But our CEOs were unanimous: the CEO must develop and own the strategy; it's part of the day job now and can't be put to one side or delegated.

Development of strategy must start with a rigorous review of eight things: customer needs, market trends, the competition, the economics of participating, positioning and capabilities, radical options, financial modelling, and execution. The aim here is to create a 360° view of your position in the market, where the market is heading, where your position could be in a changed market, taking into account developments by competitors as well as technological and other changes. Be wary of underestimating the competition, or overestimating your own business model or people: calm, objective judgement of your relative strengths and weaknesses is essential. You are then in a position to address the fundamental 'why' question of strategy – to create the corporate 'purpose' that employees can buy into – before delving into issues of how and when.

Strategy development should not be allied to budgetary decisions – conflating these issues will kill creative strategy, and won't do the budget process any favours either. Strategy is about the deep pools of profit that can sustain a company in the long term, not about performance/ operational management: 'Strategic nirvana' is pursuing sustainable competitive advantage which gives you an enduring ability to have superior performance,' says Fabio Schvartsman, CEO of Klabin.

Strategy should be done less frequently than operational reviews, but more frequently than previously. As Bill Rogers, CEO of SunTrust says: 'Things are moving so fast, we now do strategy reviews updates every six months.' The trick is to join up the dots between the different processes: Sara LaPorta, Head of Strategy for Beverages, PepsiCo, opines 'Little "s" strategies are about more day-to-day decisions which have big effects, while big "S" strategies relate to who you are and what you do. But the two need to be connected.'

Our CEOs were all agreed that there needs to be a core team of conspirators who develop strategy, a kitchen cabinet of trusted advisers, three or four 'believers'. These individuals should be in the CEO's immediate executive team in order that there is no gap between strategy development and strategy execution.

In formulating strategy the core team need to begin by asking the right question, such as 'What is our right to win, and how will we do it?' It is also essential to gather the right data – it is easy to find data that supports almost any viewpoint. Challenging the data and seeking alternative sources is a vital task.

It is helpful to provide a working hypothesis for the strategy that can be dismissed or improved upon following discussion of data and insights.

'Never let the market define you, you should define yourself.'

In formulating strategy it is always important to test that the propositions are sufficiently radical; take time to ask the impossible or impolitic questions. Use the Blue Ocean theory of strategy formulation – putting open water between yourself and your competitors to draw bold conclusions. Tom Fanning, CEO of Southern & Co, says: 'Never let the market define you, you should define yourself.'

It is vital that the strategy, once formulated, is distilled into something simple to communicate: 'Strategy should be capable of being fitted to one page – if not, it'll be too complicated to engage the organization to deliver,' argues Phil Bentley, Managing Director of British Gas. In addition, it must be quantifiable, as Jeff Holzschuh, Chairman of Institutional Securities Group, says: 'For a strategy to be effective it needs to be measurable in some way. Broad generalizations will just not do.' Cláudio Bérgamo dos Santos, CEO of Hyper Marcas, advises: 'To make strategy work you have to make it simple, communicate it well/often and review performance metrics from a strategic point of view.'

Furthermore, the strategy must be easily communicable, for if it cannot be plainly communicated, it cannot be well executed. Remember Einstein's words: if you can't explain something to a six-year-old, you don't understand it yourself.

Much of the traditional discussion of strategy and how companies should develop it is focused on what strategy is and how to formulate it. The elephant in the room is how the strategy is executed. The road to hell is paved with poor execution. Sascha Bopp, CEO of Crate and Barrel, states: 'Any strategy which ignores execution is not a strategy. How can you possibly disconnect what you are doing from where you are meant to be going?'

The CEO must lead the charge on strategy, supported by their small coterie of 'conspirators', who must believe in the strategy at least as strongly as the CEO, be loyal to the CEO and the company, behave in line with the strategy, be willing to explain the strategy (and its implications) to doubters. Next in line is the executive who will need to have the strategy explained in some detail so they can understand why it is the best alternative, and so they can get behind the strategy. They will also need to have the implications of the strategy set out both in terms of long-term and short-term goals, and in terms of who are the likely winners and losers. Then come management, who need to understand what the strategy is overall, and most especially they need to understand how their role fits into it, what they are expected to do to support the strategy and how they will be rewarded for doing so. Last, the frontline teams need to have the strategy explained simply and in terms of an overall purpose. They need to understand the importance of what they are doing and how it makes a difference. Constantino de Oliveira Jr, Chairman of GOL, says: 'Companies need to have "purpose" to guide management as to how to engage and behave. It helps to create a positive environment where people feel they can make a difference.'

Communicating the strategy and its purpose to everyone in the company is vital.

A common formulation of the frequency of communications needed to these various different constituencies is as follows: constant communications with the co-conspirators; weekly communications with the executive; monthly communications to management; and quarterly to the whole company. Where you have less frequent communication, e.g. to the further echelons of the company, you need very simplified communication. This process is the 'Ripple Theory of Engagement', whereby the further out from the inner sanctum of the co-conspirators the communications of strategy reach, the more the message has to be crafted into a simple, attractive and relevant communication.

For these communications to be effective the CEO needs to have an excellent team at their side. Money is easy, people are not.

Our CEOs were unanimous that investment in premium human capital is always worth doing, and that the choice of the top team is something that the CEO must decide for themselves. This vital task should not be delegated to HR, or to anyone else. 'Go for gold' in the top executive, and don't be afraid of losing nay-sayers. There is often too little time spent on the people side of strategy: *business strategy must be supported by people strategy*.

If the model of management in the business is the 'enabling/ empowering' one (this may not necessarily be the case), then execution of strategy should be regarded as a shared endeavour. This requires that management feed back to the top leadership team subtle changes occurring on the ground in customer behaviour, market trends, or competitors' strategies. It also requires that the top leadership team then listen to such information, such that the strategy can be kept permanently alive and refreshed, taking into account changing markets.

Using the wealth of experience of the CEOs we consulted in researching this book as well as the expertise of our partners, we uncovered the following ten strategic pitfalls companies frequently make:

- excessive short-termism
- ignoring external trends, particularly challenging ones
- overconfidence based on existing success
- failure to respond to structural changes in the market
- failure to employ the best possible team
- failure to focus and getting blown off course
- inability to foster belief in the strategy

- inability to translate the strategy into a corporate 'purpose' which employees can buy into
- failure to instil a sense of pace
- failure to create accountability for results.

By being aware of these potential bear traps, CEOs can instead focus on how to generate their opposite virtues: long-termism; being in tune with the market; humility; moving to the next business model early; meritocracy; focus; consistency; purpose; pace; and accountability.

With this in mind we have suggested the following golden rules for incoming CEOs:

- walk the corridors and meet the frontline people
- talk to the stakeholders
- work out the fundamental business model of the current business
- think radically about the business
- assess your people rigorously
- trust your judgement
- act rapidly and decisively
- search for the purpose of the business
- be clear that you understand the culture and how it works
- focus, focus, focus!

Strategy is not easy but it is straightforward. No company has an excuse any more for having a poor strategy.

While the markets have become complex, the tools for strategy are well-known and, as long as they are deployed rigorously and sensibly, then a good strategy should emerge.

But the CEO and the executive team now have to lead and to be an intimate part of the strategy process ... and not just manage it.

'The CEO must get involved.'

Even that will not guarantee strategic success as it is still possible to implement strategy poorly – and, in OC&C's opinion, most failed strategies result from implementation errors rather than poor design. Strategically high performing companies have learned how to avoid the major implementation pitfalls by following some basic rules – and, in particular, by focusing on getting and motivating the best people.

There is still no guarantee, but in this way the CEO can certainly move the odds in the company's favour.

According to Arno Mahlert, former CEO and CFO of maxingvest: 'The CEO must get involved, pose enough questions, be open to learn from others (even consultants!), be prepared to accept inconvenient truths, look for early markers of structural change and make tough decisions.'

At the end of the day, however, making strategy work is blood, sweat and tears in equal measure. You need a good team, good judgement, perhaps even a modicum of good luck ... and a brilliant strategy, of course.

Further insights: the strategy checklist

There have been a few new approaches to strategy but none of them have changed the core strategy process that most companies should pursue. The leadership need to check whether their team have completed the following tasks. Have they been able to …

Establish customer/consumer needs

Few companies now believe that they can progress without a deep insight into what their customers really think. Zhang Ruimin of white goods giant Haier Group insists, 'Every employee must listen to the customer.' As Roberto Prisco Paraiso Ramos, Chairman, Odebrecht Oil and Gas, puts it, 'At the end of the day, clients create value not companies. Everyone needs to be client oriented and making sure clients are listened to. They are the source of most new business growth ideas.'

'Every employee must listen to the customer.'

And yet many companies do not have good ways to track customer needs in a systematic way, relying on rather outdated forms of customer research rather than launching themselves into the digital world to get real time information as to how the customer is feeling now, how that has developed since last week, what is important to them, and so on.

Analyse market trends and the drivers thereof

There are many global trends and macroeconomic indicators. Few of them drive actual customer and consumer behaviour *a priori*. They may be correlated in retrospect but have limited use in terms of having the information early enough to help with forecasting demand. Microanalysis needs to be done to find useful indicators of demand and surrogate drivers for it that can be monitored and acted upon in a realistic time frame.

Investigate competitive activity

It is surprising how poorly most companies approach competitive analysis, contenting themselves with general descriptions of their competitors and often fundamentally flawed (or absent) perspectives of their economics. Seldom are these perspectives born out of factual analysis.

Despite this apparent indifference to good competitive information, there is usually a wealth of information in your own company (market analysts, previous employees of your competitors, and so on) that would allow you to analyse the economics of the competition and to do a comparative analysis of your economics versus theirs. In turn this would allow you to think through the economic consequences of your strategic options and activities. Similarly competitive gaming usually yields substantial rewards in terms of thinking through strategic options and their attractiveness.

Understand the economics of participating

Of all the elements of the strategy development process this is the one least well served by most companies. The little economic analysis that is done tends to be superficial and generally unenlightening. Too often strategists confuse the Profit and Loss (P&L) statement with the need to understand the fundamental economics of the industry, their business and their competitors.

Much of what strategy consultants have to say often comes from their preoccupation with understanding the economics of the ecosystem in which the client finds themself.

A true, cash flow based analysis can reveal much about the industry and how competition is conducted. Competitive behaviour is often much more influenced by cash flow considerations than the P&L even though the investor market seems to be preoccupied by short-term P&L performance.

How often have we heard, 'We do not understand how competitor X can afford to compete at these price levels.' Often, it is obvious. Either they believe in the value of market share (as well they should) or their cash costs/needs are much below yours – for instance, because they have not invested for many years, have no/little debt and/or are more interested in cash than profit. Relatively simple economic analysis would reveal all you need to know about the competition – and yourselves.

Interrogate your company's positioning and capabilities

All too seldom, management conduct penetrating outside-in evaluations of their own positioning and capabilities, relying instead on self-assessment. While in many cases this is done to an acceptable level, it can risk optimistic (and possibly biased or out of date) views of the company's real capabilities and competitive position. This is a bad starting point for a strategic process that is focused on defining winning sources of competitive advantage/differentiation. As Gerald Corbett, Chairman of Moneysupermarket and Britvic, among others, points out: 'You make strategic moves beyond the capability of your organization at your peril.'

In this context, there are good reasons why competitive gaming should be adopted to flush out what differentiates one competitor from the other, by giving the 'competing team' considerable resources to create winning strategies versus the 'home team'.

This is a common feature of the defence and security world, where such programmes are at the core of ensuring the defensibility of the strategies adopted by companies and, indeed, countries. It should become a common feature of corporate strategy development processes.

Elaborate radical (and not so radical) options

One of the major risks in all strategy processes is that the process homes in too early on a single outcome – maybe the CEO's hypothesis (or prejudice) – at the cost of a thorough evaluation of the attractiveness and risk of other courses of action.

Indeed it is entirely normal that the board or supervisory committee of a company only ever is presented with the final answer to the strategy question rather than the list of options that have been considered (thoroughly) and why they have been discarded. Providing more information about the options would allow them to be debated and understood.

This debate about strategic options – which would be entirely appropriate – would improve the quality of thinking about the chosen option, increasing the conviction about, and commitment to, the resulting outcome.

And the options should include a few radical ones just to test the validity of a business-as-usual strategy, which might be right but which needs to be tested fully just to ensure that it is not the product of the inertia, the lack of creativity or, worse still, the lack of ambition of the management team. Generally, strategy processes need to be radicalized even if the resulting strategy is a 'no change' strategy.

Compare financial models of the options facing the company

All options and trade-offs need to be manifested in a single framework so that they can be compared and evaluated. The chosen framework of most companies is the financial one. With a little thought, and based upon a good economic analysis (see above), it is relatively straightforward to express options in comparative economic/financial terms.

By risk-weighting the options, it is also possible to compare different options as to their likely 'expected outcome' and hence make more informed choices. Even if it is difficult to establish risk it is still possible to have a debate about 'what would you have to believe for this option to be attractive'.

A simple approach but one infrequently encountered.

Prioritize and choose, bearing in mind risk and competitive reaction

If the financials are done in an insightful way (see the previous point) then this step becomes trivial as the attractiveness of the various choices tends to become clear. Debating the options, however, is critical as this has a number of important side effects:

- Refinement of the critical assumptions as more is known, understood or debated
- Engagement of the team with the options
- Buy-in of the team to the resulting strategic option
- Elaboration of the implementation/execution challenges

Elaborate the implementation plan for the chosen option

This is probably the most straightforward of all the steps in a good strategy process. If all the groundwork is done well in the previous steps, then this step almost logically falls out. Much of the thinking will have already been done even though it may still require documentation and the elaboration of some of the detail, e.g., pushing down into the operational implications for the day-to-day activities of the 'frontline staff' as it may be that the strategy will stand or fall on the way the staff deliver 'customer service' as a crucial differentiator from competitors.

* * *

This rather generic strategy development process remains fundamentally unchanged compared to 25 years ago and if you wish to test how you are doing then you can always apply McKinsey's very helpful 'Ten Timeless Tests'.[1]

1. Will your strategy beat the market?
2. Does the strategy tap the true source of advantage?
3. Is the strategy granular about where to compete?
4. Does the strategy put the enterprise ahead of trends and discontinuities?
5. Does the strategy embed privileged insight and foresight?
6. Is uncertainty properly defined and accounted for?
7. Does the strategy balance high-commitment choices with flexibility and learning?
8. Have alternatives been evaluated without bias or false inference?
9. Is there true conviction to act?
10. Is the strategy translated into clear actions and reallocation of resources?

As we have said earlier, the science and technology of developing strategy is no longer a mystery. The tools, techniques and indeed the process are well-known. What is less evident is how to assure that they are prosecuted vigorously and effectively. You need competent and experienced people at the helm of these all-important processes, working for the CEO and accountable to the corporation.

At the risk of repeating ourselves, strategy development is straightforward but not easy!

Endnotes

Chapter 2. Developing good strategy – a science or an art?

1. Richard Koch, *FT Guide to Strategy: How to Create, Pursue and Deliver a Winning Strategy* (Harlow: Pearson Education Ltd, 4th edn, 2011).
2. This approach contrasts with the traditional Red Ocean approach, which takes its name from the blood that spills into the water when companies struggle for market share in established markets. W. Chan Kim and Renée Mauborgne, *Blue Ocean Strategy: How to Create Uncontested Market Space and Make the Competition Irrelevant* (Boston, MA: Harvard Business School Press, 2005).
3. OC&C, *The Strategic Promised Land: Winning Using End-Game Strategies*, www.occstrategy.nl/our-capabilities/our-sectors/global-strategic-thinking/ publications/strategic-promised-land.
4. Babette Bensoussan and Craig Fleisher, *Analysis without Paralysis: 10 Tools to Make Better Strategic Decisions* (Harlow: FT/Prentice Hall, 2008).
5. OC&C, *Strategy Hypothesis Survey: Key Findings*, July 2012.
6. Depressingly, Bain & Co.'s annual 'Management Tools & Trends' survey of up to 11,000 respondents repeatedly ranks benchmarking as one of the most popular tools used by managers. Certainly, benchmarking has its place, but its extreme popularity is mystifying. In the words of one of the CEOs we interviewed: 'I have prohibited our staff from benchmarking. It's for losers. Why would I want

to manage to an industry average?' John Goodwin, CFO of The LEGO Group, reinforces the message: 'Avoid death by benchmarking,' he says. 'It's a middle management preoccupation.' Bain & Co., *Management Tools 2011: An Executive's Guide* (2011), www.bain.com/publications/articles/management-tools-2011-executives-guide.aspx.

Chapter 3. What makes strategy development difficult nowadays?

1 There have been other attempts to explain the course of globalization using the software industry's system for labelling product iterations. In *The World Is Flat* (2005), Thomas Friedman suggested the existence of Globalization 1.0 (kicking off with Columbus in 1492 and lasting until around the end of the 18th century); Globalization 2.0 (an era in which change was driven by large corporations, which persisted until 2000) and Globalization 3.0 (an era in which software and the internet are continuing to 'flatten' the world, enabling competitive threats to emerge from all angles). Friedman describes waiting for a flight at an airport and understanding all of these transitions in terms of a plane ticket: 'In Globalization 1.0, there was a ticket agent. In Globalization 2.0, the e-ticket machine replaced the ticket agent. In Globalization 3.0, you are your own ticket agent.' Thomas Friedman, *The World Is Flat: A Brief History of the Twenty-First Century* (New York: Farrar Straus and Giroux, 2005).

2 H. Kharas, 'The Emerging Middle Class in Developing Countries', OECD Development Centre Working Paper No. 285 (Paris: OECD, 2010).

3 'Flat-Panel Displays: Cracking Up', *The Economist*, 17 January 2012, www.economist.com/blogs/schumpeter/2012/01/flat-panel-displays-0.

4 Strategy Analytics, 'Apple iPhone Generates US$150bn of Revenues since Launch', 27 June 2012, www.marketwatch.com/story/strategy-analytics-apple-iphone-generates-us150-billion-of-revenues-since-launch-2012-06-27; Horace Dediu, 'How Many iPhone "5s" Will Be Sold?', *Asymco*, 6 August 2012, www.asymco.com/2012/08/06/how-many-of-the-next-generation-of-iphone-will-be-sold.

5 OC&C, *Strategy Hypothesis Survey: Key Findings*, July 2012.

6 OC&C, *Strategy Hypothesis Survey: Key Findings*, July 2012.

7 Richard Koch, and Greg Lockwood, *Superconnect: How the Best Connections in Business and Life are the Ones You Least Expect* (New York: W. W. Norton & Co., 2010).

8 'The New Workplace Currency – It's Not Just Salary Anymore: Cisco Study Highlights New Rules for Attracting Young Talent into the Workplace', 2 November 2011, http://newsroom.cisco.com/press-releasecontent?type=webcontent&articleId=532138.

9 OC&C, *Strategy Hypothesis Survey: Key Findings*, July 2012.

10 OC&C, *Strategy Hypothesis Survey: Key Findings*, July 2012.

Chapter 4. Why the top team must lead the charge

1 OC&C, *Strategy Hypothesis Survey: Key Findings*, July 2012.

Chapter 6. So how do managers make a difference to strategy?

1 http://www.entrepreneur.com/article/225967.

Chapter 7. Ten strategic pitfalls …

1 Phil Rosenzweig, *The Halo Effect … and the Eight Other Business Delusions that Deceive Managers* (New York: Free Books, 2007).

2 Kurt Eichenwald, 'Microsoft's Lost Decade', *Vanity Fair*, August 2012.

3 According to Tony Lewin, author of *Smart Thinking: The Little Car That Made It Big*, Mercedes started work on city car proposals in the late 1970s and early 1980s under the direction of Johann Tomforde, a young designer based in Stuttgart. During the late 1980s, Tomforde's ideas found an echo in Swatch inventor Nicolas Hayek's effort to design a small and stylish city car called the Swatchmobile. (Hayek actually went on to hire Tomforde, putting him in charge of the Swatchmobile project.) In 1994, Mercedes' parent company Daimler-Benz partnered with SMH, the watch manufacturer run by Hayek, acquiring a 51% stake in the joint venture company that would produce Tomforde's designs. After the launch of the first Smart car models in 1998, Daimler-Benz acquired full control of the joint venture. Lewin outlines the scepticism with which Mercedes initially regarded Hayek's efforts: 'Small cars meant small profits ... anything other than a standard petrol powertrain meant a lot of expense, a lot of inconvenience and a lot of future warranty-cost risk, and ... it was impossible to sell environmental friendliness, in the market-place, especially to small car customers with little cash.' Tony Lewin, *Smart Thinking: The Little Car That Made It Big* (St Paul, MN: Motorbooks, 2004).

Further insights: the strategy checklist

1 Chris Bradley, Martin Hirt and Sven Smit, 'Have You Tested Your Strategy Lately?', *McKinsey Quarterly*, January 2011.

Contributor biographies

Phil Bentley was the Managing Director of British Gas, the top energy and services provider to British homes and businesses, from March 2007 until early 2013. Previously, he was Group Finance Director and Managing Director, Europe of Centrica plc. He joined Centrica in November 2000 from Diageo, where he was Global Finance Director for Guinness-UDV. Prior to that he was Group Treasurer and Director of Risk Management of Diageo plc. Previously, he spent 15 years in senior finance roles at BP, many of which were spent in BP's exploration businesses in China, the US and Egypt. He holds a Master's Degree from Pembroke College, Oxford University, and has an MBA from INSEAD in France. He was a fellow of the Chartered Institute of Management Accountants and a member of the Association of Corporate Treasurers. He has recently joined the Board of IMI plc, one of the UK's leading engineering groups.

Rob van den Bergh is Chairman of the Supervisory Board of NV Deli Universal and Isala Clinics. He is also a member of the Supervisory Board of Ahold, Postcodeloterjj, TomTom and Pon. Rob is also a member of the Advisory Board of CVC Capital Partners BV and a member of the Investment Committee of NPM Capital NV. He had a longstanding career with VNU NV (currently Nielsen Media Research BV) from 1980 to 2006, finally as the Chairman of the Executive Board in the US.

Richard Bielle was Chairman of the Management Board of CFAO until September 2012 and was also a member of the company's Executive Committee. Before being appointed to this position in 2009, he was the Director of Operations and Development for the group's automotive division. He joined CFAO in 1999 as Director of Development in charge of automotive operations then in 2002 became Secretary General of the group, in charge of finance. A graduate of Ecole Supérieure de Commerce de Paris, he began his career in the financial sector. In 1988, he joined Renault Trucks and held various positions within its finance department. In 1997, he joined ING Barings as a Senior Manager, heading up project financing.

Patrick Boissier serves as the Chairman and CEO of DCNS Group, Alstom Leroux Naval and Ateliers de Montoir. He has been President of the Marine Sector of ALSTOM Deutschland AG and Alstom SA since August 1998. He also serves as the Chief Operating Officer of Cegelec SA and Cegelec B.V.

Sascha Bopp joined Crate and Barrel in 2009 as Chief Operating Officer, and was appointed CEO in 2012. He oversees all three brands under the Crate and Barrel umbrella: Crate and Barrel, CB2 and The Land of Nod. Prior to joining Crate and Barrel, he was Managing Director and CFO at Primondo GmbH, a $5 billion German multichannel retailer. He was also CEO of Primondo's Specialty Group division. Earlier in his career, Sascha spent six years in the private equity sector at The Invus Group in Paris and six years in strategy consulting in Boston.

John F. Brock has been Chairman of Coca-Cola Enterprises Inc. since 2008 and has been the company's CEO since 2006. From 2003 until 2005, he was CEO of InBev SA and from 1999 until 2002 he was COO of Cadbury Schweppes plc. He was named Beverage Industry Executive of the Year in 2000, has served as Director of Dow Jones & Company, Reed Elsevier plc. and Campbell Soup, and serves on the Georgia Tech Foundation Board and on the Board of Visitors for Owen Business School.

Sir George Buckley joined Arle Capital LLP when he retired from 3M where he was Chairman, President and CEO from 2005 to 2012. Prior to that, Sir George was Chairman and CEO of Brunswick Corporation from 2000 to 2005. He also held senior general management roles at Emerson and British Railways. Sir George is an engineer by training and holds a PhD in electrical engineering along with four honorary Doctorates and approximately 20 patents. He is Chairman of Arle Capital LLP, Chairman of Expro International and a Non-Executive Director of Technogym. In addition, he is a Member of the Board of Directors of PepsiCo, Hitachi, Archer Daniels Midland and Stanley Black & Decker. He also sits on the Americas Advisory Board for Deutsche Bank and the Advisory Board for Rothschild North America.

Jørgen Buhl Rasmussen is President and CEO of Carlsberg A/S, one of the world's leading brewers. Prior to taking up this post he had an extensive career in consumer products companies including Master Foods, Duracell and Gillette. Immediately prior to Carlsberg he was President of Gillette's Africa, Middle East and Eastern Europe business.

Sumit Chandwani is co-founder and Managing Partner of Arth Capital. Prior to establishing the Indian-based investment fund in early 2012 he was an executive director of ICICI Venture. Sumit has 20 years of experience in private equity and structured finance. In 2010 he was awarded the *Asian Venture Capital Journal* Indian Private Equity Professional of the Year.

Michel Combes is CEO, Northern and Central Europe, of Vodafone. He joined the company in October 2008. From 2006 to 2008 he was Chairman and CEO of TDF Group. From 2003 to 2006 Michel held senior positions with France Telecom Group, where he started his career in 1986. He was Executive Vice-President of Nouvelles Frontières Group from 1999 until the end of 2001, when he moved to the position of CEO of Assystem-Brime, a company specializing in industrial engineering. After being technical advisor to the Minister of Transportation from 1991 to 1995, he served as Chairman and CEO of GlobeCast from 1995 to 1999.

Gerald Corbett is currently Chairman of Betfair, Britvic, Moneysupermarket.com Group and the Royal National Institute for the Deaf (Action on Hearing Loss). He is also a Non-Executive Director of the investment and stock broking business, Numis Securities, and of Towry Holdings. Gerald's previous roles include Chairman of SSL International between 2005 and 2010, Chairman of The Woolworths Group between 2001 and 2007, Chief Executive of Railtrack, Group Finance Director of Grand Metropolitan and Group Finance Director of Redland.

Patrick Coveney joined the Board of Greencore in September 2005 as CFO, becoming CEO in April 2008. Prior to that he was a partner with McKinsey and Company, serving as Managing Partner of McKinsey, Ireland. He is also President of the Dublin Chamber of Commerce.

Gavin Darby was appointed CEO of Premier Foods in February 2013. He spent 15 years at the Coca-Cola Company in various senior positions, including Division President roles for North West Europe and Central Europe. Prior to joining Premier Foods, Gavin served as CEO of Cable & Wireless Worldwide plc., leading a successful turnaround of the business before negotiating its eventual sale to Vodafone plc. Previously he worked at Vodafone plc. for nine years, during which time he served as UK CEO and CEO of Americas, Africa, India and China. Earlier in his career Gavin held various sales and marketing roles in SC Johnson and Spillers Foods. He graduated with a degree in Management Science from the University of Manchester. Gavin served as a non-executive director for Intertek plc. between 2009 and 2011.

Thierry de la Tour d'Artaise was appointed Chairman and CEO of SEB in 2000. He joined Groupe SEB in 1994, becoming Managing Director and then Chairman of Calor before being appointed Deputy Chairman of SEB SA in 1999. He was then appointed President of the Home Equipment Division. Thierry began his career in the United States as Financial Controller at Allendale Insurance Johnson before spending four years with Coopers & Lybrand as Audit Manager in Paris. Afterwards he joined Groupe Chargeurs, holding different positions in the finance department before serving as CFO and later as CEO of Croisières Paquet. He holds a degree from the Ecole Supérieure de Commerce de Paris, and is a chartered accountant.

Romulo de Mello Dias has been Cielo CEO since May 2008, and was a member of the Cielo Board from 2005 to May 2008. Cielo is the leading company in the merchant acquiring and payment processing industry in Brazil, with net revenue of US$ 2.9 billion in 2012. Romulo previously worked at Bradesco BBI and as an executive director at Citibank, Bradespar and other companies. He was a managing partner at Albion Alliance Capital and a member of the Board of Directors of Companhia Vale do Rio Doce, Valepar, Escelsa, Enersul, Net, Americel, Telet, Even, Monteiro Aranha, Alelo and CPM. Over the course of his career, Romulo has developed an extensive background in business management through his experience in private equity.

Alexis Duval was appointed CEO of Tereos in 2012. Previously, he was the Chief Financial Officer of Tereos and CEO of Tereos Internacional. Alexis has spent more than ten years in executive positions within the group after joining Franco Brasileira SA AcÀucar e Alcool (FBA), a joint venture between Tereos and Brazilian group Cosan in 2002. Alexis began his career in the US at Sucres et Denrées.

Frits van Eerd is CEO of the privately held Jumbo Supermarkten, founded by his father Karel van Eerd. Before being appointed CEO in 1996, Frits held a number of positions in the company, starting his career as a regular PoS employee. He was awarded 'Influencer of the Year' in 2012 and 'Topman van het Jaar' in 2009 after the successful acquisition of Super de Boer and C1000. Jumbo is now the second largest supermarket chain in the Netherlands.

Thomas A. Fanning is Chairman, President and CEO of Southern Company, one of America's largest electricity producers. He has worked in the company for more than 30 years, holding 15 different positions in eight different business units, serving as Chief Operating Officer in his last role before his appointment to his current position in 2010. Prior to this he was the company's CFO, responsible for accounting, finance, tax, investor relations, treasury and risk management functions. He has also served as President and CEO of Gulf Power. In addition to his role at Southern Company, he serves on the Board of Directors of the Federal Reserve Bank of Atlanta and the Georgia Tech College of Management Advisory Board, and the Board of Trustees for the Georgia Tech Foundation. He is also a member of the Business Roundtable and co-chairs the group's North American Energy Policy Development Committee.

David Feffer is the CEO of Suzano Holding and was appointed Chairman of the Board of Directors of Suzano Papel e Celulose in 2001. With more than 85 years' experience, the Suzano Group is one of the soundest private organizations in Brazil, with strong participation in the pulp, paper and renewable energy industries, as well as activities in other segments. The Group presented net revenue of US$2.7 billion in 2012. David joined the Suzano Group in 1974, where he held several executive positions.

Murilo Ferreira has been the CEO of Vale, a world leading mining company, since 2011. Vale is one of the largest Brazilian firms with net revenue of more than US$46 billion and 136,400 employees worldwide. Prior to that, Mr Murilo was Vale's Executive Officer with responsibility over several different departments from 2005 to 2008, including aluminium, coal, stakes in steel projects, energy, new business, mergers and acquisitions, nickel and base metals. He served as CEO of Vale Canada from 2007 to 2008, and has also been CEO of Alunorte, Albras and Mineração Vera Cruz. He has also been a Member of the Board of Directors of several other companies, including Usiminas, and was a partner at Studio Investimentos, an asset management firm.

Dean Finch is Group Chief Executive of National Express, a leading transport provider delivering services in the UK, North America, Spain and Morocco. Prior to joining National Express in 2009, Dean was Group Chief Executive of Tube Lines. Before that he worked for more than ten years in senior roles within FirstGroup plc. He joined FirstGroup in 1999 having qualified as a Chartered Accountant with KPMG, where he worked for 12 years specializing in Corporate Transaction Support Services. At FirstGroup, he held various positions in the UK and North America, starting as Managing Director of the Rail Division and becoming Group Chief Operating Officer.

Stuart Fletcher was appointed Chief Executive of Bupa in March 2012. From 2004 until 2011, he was President of Diageo International and has held a number of senior management positions at Diageo since joining the company in 1986, including Global Finance Director of Guinness. Previously Stuart held various financial positions with Procter & Gamble.

Jerry Fowden has been the CEO of the Cott Corporation since 2009. He joined the company in 2007 and held several international management positions. Previously, he served as CEO of Trader Media Group and as a member of its parent Guardian Media Group's board of directors from 2005 until 2007. Prior to that he worked in a variety of roles with ABInBev.

Nadir Godrej is the Managing Director of Godrej Industries and Chairman of Godrej Agrovet. He is also a Director of numerous firms, including Godrej & Boyce, Godrej Foods and Godrej Consumer Products. Currently, Nadir is the President of the Indo French Technical Association and the Alliance Française Mumbai. For his contribution to Indo-French relations, the French Government has honoured him with the Chevalier de L'Ordre National du Mérite and the National Order of the Legion of Honour.

John Goodwin is the Chief Financial Officer of The LEGO Group. Prior to joining LEGO in 2012, he was a President with Procter & Gamble, where he led a number of the company's global businesses.

Andy Green was appointed CEO of Logica in 2008 and held that position until the acquisition of the company by CGI in 2012. Previously, he had been the head of the global services division of BT as well as Chief Strategy Officer.

Antonio Carlos Guimarães has been Syngenta's Regional Director for Latin America for the past nine years. He previously served as CFO for Brazil and Latam. He also was, during the period 2010–2012, President of Crop Life Latin America Board of Directors, the industry association for Crop Protection. Prior to that, Antonio held several executive positions, including CFO for LVMH (Louis Vuitton Moet Hennessy) Brazil for six years, and CIO in a Brazilian fertilizer company.

Dr Kurt-Ludwig Gutberlet has been CEO of BSH since 2001. Earlier, he held several international managerial positions in the company, which he joined in the business sector planning department in 1983. He holds a doctoral degree from Kiel University and worked as a research assistant at the Kiel Institute for the World Economy.

Tom Hall is a Partner and Co-Head of the media team of Apax Partners, based in the London office. Tom has both led and participated in a number of key deals including The Stationery Office, Zeneus Pharma and Thomson Directories. He has served as advisor and board member to a number of Apax portfolio companies including Truvo, Trader Media Group and SouFun. Prior to joining Apax Partners in 1998, Tom was a Media Analyst at Deutsche Morgan Grenfell and he began his career with SG Warburg, also as a Media Analyst.

Rick Hamada was named CEO of Avnet, Inc., in February 2011. He joined the firm in 1983 as a technical specialist. His career evolved to encompass sales and marketing roles, including serving as a Field Sales Representative, Computer Sales Manager, Sales Unit Director, Regional Sales Manager, Area Vice-President, and Vice-President of Business Development for Open Systems. In 2006, he became Chief Operating Officer, in which role he spearheaded efforts to drive profitable growth through enterprise initiatives focused on operational excellence, employee engagement and customer engagement. He was promoted to President and Chief Operating Officer in May 2010. In September 2012, he was named chairman of the Global Technology Distribution Council, an industry consortium representing the world's leading IT distributors. He holds a BSc from San Diego State University, where in June 2009 he was named a member of the advisory board of its College of Business Administration.

Michael E. Hansen was appointed as CEO of Cengage Learning in September 2012. Before joining Cengage, he served as CEO of Elsevier Health Sciences, a division of Reed Elsevier, and before that as President and CEO of Harcourt Assessment, which was then the education arm of Reed Elsevier. He has also been the Executive Vice-President of Operational Excellence at Bertelsmann, a $20 billion global media company, and has served briefly as head of international operations at Proxicom, an internet-focused technology company. He spent the first 11 years of his career with the Boston Consulting Group in New York, ultimately becoming Partner and Co-Chairman of e-Business and Media Practice.

Barney Harford serves as CEO of Orbitz Worldwide. He also serves as a director on the Orbitz Worldwide board of directors. He joined Orbitz Worldwide, one of the world's leading online travel companies, in January 2009. Previously, he served in a variety of roles at Expedia, Inc. from 1999 to 2006. From 2004 to 2006, he served as President of Expedia Asia Pacific, leading the company's entry into China, Japan and Australia. Prior to Expedia, Barney worked in the United Kingdom as a strategy consultant with The Kalchas Group. He now also serves as a Board member of LiquidPlanner, an on-demand project management service that is transforming the way organizations manage complex projects.

Andy Harrison was appointed Chief Executive of Whitbread in 2010. He served as Chief Executive of easyJet from 2005 to 2010 and was Chief Executive of RAC (previously Lex Services) from 1996 to 2005. Prior to this he held the roles of Managing Director of Courtaulds International Fabrics and Finance Director of Courtaulds Textiles. In the past, Andy also held a Non-Executive Directorship at Emap, where he was Chairman of the Audit Committee.

Cees 't Hart became CEO of Royal FrieslandCampina in 2009. He joined the company after having held several international management positions at Unilever, where he joined as a management trainee in 1984. He is also Chairman of NZO, Member of Executive Committee VNO-NCW and Chairman of Topsector Agrifood Platform in the Netherlands advising the Dutch government.

Jan Michiel Hessels is the Chairman of the NYSE Euronext Board of Directors and served as Chairman of the Supervisory Board of Euronext from its creation in 2000 until the merger of Euronext and NYSE Group in 2007. He is currently also the Chairman of the supervisory board of Boskalis and was the Chairman of the supervisory board of Philips as well as a member of the supervisory board of Heineken. Jan Michiel was the CEO of Royal Vendex KBB from 1990 to 2000.

Dr Rainer Hillebrand was appointed Vice-CEO of the Otto Group in 2007. He has been a member of the company's Executive Board since 1999. He joined the company as the Head of Strategy Development in 1990. Prior to that Rainer was an independent consultant. He holds a doctoral degree from the University of the German Federal Armed Forces, which he entered after having become an officer.

Jeffrey R. Holzschuh is Chairman of Institutional Securities Group and a member of the firm's Management Committee. In addition, he is the Chairman of Morgan Stanley's Global Power and Utility Group, where he also serves as Chairman of the Environmental Policy Committee and as President of its investment in venture capital business. He has been appointed by the US Secretary of Energy to serve on the US Electricity Advisory Board and has previously served as Chair of the EEI Wall Street Advisory Group.

He is a founding member of the US Partnership for Renewable Energy Finance.

Philippe Houzé was appointed Chairman and CEO of Groupe Galeries Lafayette in 2005. From 1998, he was a Co-President of the company, having previously built a successful career at Monoprix, where he joined as an intern in 1969 and became General Manager in 1982 then Chairman and CEO in 1994.

Anthony Hucker became President of Giant Food in October 2011. Previously, he was on the executive team at Walmart, after joining Walmart International in 2004 as Chief Information Office of the Americas. He held various leadership positions within the company, culminating as Corporate Vice-President of Walmart Stores, Inc., and head of Strategy and Business Development. Prior to this, Anthony spent ten years with Aldi, where he served in a variety of leadership assignments in Germany, Austria and the US, and became Chief Operating Officer of Aldi UK, which he helped to launch. He is on the Self Help Africa Board of Directors and serves as a Board Member of Our Family Foundation, supporting local charities to improve the lives of children, fight hunger and help build healthy communities. He is a guest lecturer in retailing at Oxford University's Said School of Business UK, Brigham Young University's Marriott School of Business and the University of Chicago's Booth School of Business.

Penny Hughes joined the RBS Board as a Non-Executive Director in January 2010 and is currently Chair of the Group Remuneration Committee. She is also a Non-Executive Director of Wm Morrison Supermarkets plc. and a Trustee of the British Museum. She received a CBE for services to the media in the Queen's Birthday Honours list in June 2011. Penny's former Non-Executive Directorships include Cable & Wireless Worldwide plc., Home Retail Group plc.,

Gap Inc., Vodafone plc., Reuters plc., and Skandinavika Enskilda Banken AB (SEB). She is also former President of the Advertising Association. Penny spent the majority of her executive career at Coca-Cola where she held a number of leadership positions during the merger of Coca-Cola and Schweppes in the UK. In 1992 she was appointed as President, Coca-Cola Great Britain and Ireland.

M. Douglas Ivester is President and owner of Deer Run Investments, LLC. He served as the tenth chair of the board and CEO of The Coca-Cola Company from 1997 to 2000. He joined The Coca-Cola Company in 1979 as Assistant Controller and Director of Corporate Auditing, then became the youngest Vice-President in the company's history in 1981. In 1985 he was elected Chief Financial Officer. M. Douglas graduated cum laude from the University of Georgia with a BBA, then joined the Atlanta office of Ernst and Ernst, leading its team for The Coca-Cola Company. He is a member of the board of directors of SunTrust Banks, Inc., where he serves as the Lead Director. He is also a member of the boards of SunTrust Banks of Georgia and Capella Hotel Group LLC. He is Chairman of the Board of Trustees of the Woodruff Health Science Center of Emory University, where he is also Trustee. He is a member of the Governing Board of the Woodruff Arts Center of Atlanta.

Luke Jensen was appointed Group Development Director of Sainsbury's in 2011. He joined the company and the Operating Board in 2008 as Director of Strategy. He was appointed to the position of Managing Director Non-Food in 2009 with responsibility for Clothing, General Merchandise and Entertainment. Previous roles include Director/Partner and Head of the Consumer and Retail Practice of OC&C Strategy Consultants and Founder and Group FD/Executive Director of M8 Group.

Barry Judge is Chief Marketing Officer at LivingSocial. In January 2013 he joined the company, where he oversees online and offline advertising, brand management, social media, and communications. Prior to his latest post, Barry served as Best Buy's Chief Marketing Officer and Executive Vice-President for Marketing and Strategy, leading the company's omnichannel customer experience design and digital marketing initiatives. Before his 13 years with Best Buy, he was Vice-President of Marketing and Product Development at Caribou Coffee, where he was a member of the company's start up team. Barry has also held various marketing and product positions at Young & Rubicam, Coca-Cola USA, the Quaker Oats Company, and the Pillsbury Company. Barry earned his MBA from Northwestern University's Kellogg School of Management and is a graduate of Brown University.

Laura Shapira Karet became CEO in January 2012 of Giant Eagle, Inc., one of the United States's largest food retailers and distributors, with more than 35,000 team members and approximately $9.9 billion in annual sales. Prior to this, Karet served as Chief Strategy Officer and Senior Executive Vice-President. In that role, she developed and managed Giant Eagle's strategic business plans, set the direction for the company's corporate priorities, and was responsible for its manufacturing ventures. Karet joined Giant Eagle in 2000 as Vice-President of Marketing, and was later promoted to Senior Vice-President of Marketing and President of New Formats. She received the 2011 Ernst & Young Entrepreneur of the Year Western Pennsylvania and West Virginia Award. She was also recognized as one of *Progressive Grocer* magazine's 2010 Top Women in Grocery. Prior to joining Giant Eagle, Karet held marketing executive positions at Sara Lee from 1997 to 2000 and served in several brand management roles at Procter & Gamble from 1990 to 1997.

Justin King was appointed CEO of Sainsbury's in 2004. He is also Chairman of the Operating Board. Justin was formerly Director of Food at Marks & Spencer Group and prior to this held a number of senior positions at ASDA/Walmart and Häagen Dazs UK. He spent much of his early career with Mars Confectionery and Pepsi International. In addition, Justin has been a Non-Executive Director of Staples, Inc. since September 2007 and was appointed to the board of the London Organising Committee of the Olympic Games and Paralympic Games in January 2009.

Eric Kintz is Senior Vice-President and General Manager of Logitech for Business, the group within Logitech focused on unified communications and video collaboration solutions. In this role, he is responsible for product research and development, as well as worldwide marketing and sales, for unified communications solutions. He is also responsible for driving and maintaining deep partner relationships with the unified communications groups at Cisco and Microsoft. Previously, Eric was Vice-President and General Manager of Logitech's video business unit, responsible for Logitech's award-winning line of high-definition webcams. He joined Logitech in 2009 as the Vice-President of Strategy and Corporate Development. He led the development of Logitech's long-term strategy for future growth and spearheaded the acquisition of LifeSize Communications. Prior to joining Logitech, Eric was Vice-President of Strategy and Marketing for Hewlett Packard's Web Services and Software division. He was previously Vice-President of Global Marketing Strategy for HP and was recognized by *Brandweek* in 2007 as one of the top ten marketers under 40. Eric graduated from ESSEC Business School in Paris, France, with a Master of Science in Management.

Donald R. Knauss was appointed Chairman and CEO of the Clorox Company in 2006, following two years as the Executive Vice-President of The Coca-Cola Company and President and Chief

Operating Officer for Coca-Cola North America. Previously he was President of the Retail Division of Coca-Cola North America and President and CEO of The Minute Maid Company, a division of The Coca-Cola Company. Prior to his employment with Coca-Cola, he held various positions in marketing and sales with PepsiCo, Inc. and Procter & Gamble. He is also a Director of the Kellogg Company and URS Corporation.

Bernd Kundrun is a member of the Supervisory Board of RTL Group. He was the CEO of Gruner + Jahr from 2000 until 2009. Previously, he held various positions at Gruner + Jahr's and RTL's common parent, the Bertelsmann Group, which he joined in 1984 as an assistant to the Board of Bertelsmann Club. After leaving Gruner + Jahr, Bernd founded the venture capital group Hanse Ventures.

Dr Rolf Kunisch was CEO of Beiersdorf from 1994 until 2005 and member of the company's Supervisory Board from 2005 until 2011. He joined the Board of Beiersdorf in 1991 after having held different international positions at Procter & Gamble where he joined in 1968 as a product management assistant. Rolf holds a doctoral degree from the University of Cologne.

Claus-Dietrich Lahrs was appointed CEO of Hugo Boss in 2008. From 2003 until 2008, he was the Managing Director of Christian Dior Couture. Prior to that he held several management positions at Louis Vuitton, spending the last five years as CEO of the America region. Before that he was responsible for marketing and sales for Cartier's Northern Europe region.

Martin Lamb has been Chief Executive of IMI plc. since 2001, having been appointed to the Board in 1996. He has worked for IMI for more than 30 years and has held a number of senior management roles across the group during this time. Martin is also a Non-Executive Director of Severn Trent Water plc. and was formerly a Non-Executive Director of Spectris plc.

Sara LaPorta is the SVP, Global Beverages Strategy and Business Development for PepsiCo. She is responsible for providing strategic thought leadership in the areas of consumer foresight and insight across the entire GBG sector, and for developing integrated strategic frameworks and establishing common consumer insight methodologies, infrastructures, tools and capabilities across the PAB portfolio. Previously she was Executive Vice President and Chief Strategy Officer for Interactive Corporation's Retail Group. From 2002 to 2005, Sara served as SVP, Strategy & Chief Strategy Officer for Sears Roebuck & Co. Prior to this, Sara was a Vice President at The Boston Consulting Group. During her 14-year tenure at BCG, she developed growth strategies and business improvement initiatives for companies in the retail and packaged goods sector as well as in healthcare and pharmaceuticals. She holds a PhD in plant pathology and biotechnology, and in the U.S. she attended M.I.T.'s Sloan School for her MBA.

Peter Lau has been Chairman and Chief Executive of Giordano Group since 1994. He had more than 12 years of management and accounting experience in the private and public sectors in Canada before joining the group in 1987. Peter is also an Independent Non-Executive Director of Fairwood Holdings Limited which is listed on the Stock Exchange of Hong Kong.

James Lawrence is Chairman of Rothschild North America and Co-Head of Global Investment Banking. Jim is one of the founding partners and former Chairman of the LEK Partnership and joined Rothschild in 2010 from Unilever where he held the position of Executive Director and Chief Financial Officer; prior to that he was Vice-Chairman at General Mills, having also spent time in the US and in Europe in senior executive positions with Northwest

Airlines, PepsiCo, Bain & Company and The Boston Consulting Group.

Sir Terence P. Leahy has been a senior advisor at Clayton Dubilier & Rice since 2011 and is based in London. In his 32-year career at Tesco plc., Sir Terry helped to transform the company into the third-largest retailer in the world, serving in a number of senior positions, including CEO from 1997 to 2011. He was honoured with a Doctor of Science from Cranfield University in June 2007.

Ian Livingston was appointed Chief Executive of BT Group in June 2008. Previously, he was Chief Executive of BT Retail and Finance Director for BT Group. Before joining BT, Ian was Group Finance Director of the Dixons Group from 1997. He joined Dixons in 1991 and his career with the electrical retailer spanned a number of operational and financial roles, both in the UK and overseas. Earlier in his career Ian worked for 3i Group and the Bank of America International.

Guilherme Loureiro is Senior Vice President of Walmart Brasil. In his previous 24 years with Unilever, he held a variety of leadership roles across Finance, Operations, General Management and Business Development, working in Brazil, Chile, Mexico, England and the United States. In his last position at Unilever, he served as Senior Vice President, Corporate Strategies, Business Development and President of Unilever Ventures. Guilherme graduated with a bachelor's degree in Business Administration from Fundação Getulio Vargas (FGV), Sao Paulo, Brazil. He also holds a master's and doctorate in Business Administration from FGV and participated in a development program at Harvard Business School in Boston, Mass.

Gary Lubner was appointed CEO of Belron in May 2000 after having been with the company for more than 20 years. During his time with the company, Gary has held a number of roles that have seen him responsible for the growth and development of key areas of the business. Before being appointed as CEO, Gary was responsible for all of the European operations of Belron, prior to that he was Managing Director of the UK business Autoglass.

Dr Arno Mahlert is Chairman of the Supervisory Board of GfK SE and holds a number of positions on Supervisory Boards of other German companies, e.g. maxingvest ag. He was the CEO of maxingvest ag from 2007 to 2009 after having been appointed CFO of the company in 2004. Prior to that he was CFO of Verlagsgruppe Georg von Holtzbrinck from 1988 until 2003. Earlier, he held different management positions with Bertelsmann.

Jez Maiden has been Group Finance Director of National Express since 2008. He was formerly CFO at Northern Foods. Prior to that he was Group Finance Director of British Vita, Director of Finance of Britannia Building Society and Group Finance Director of Hickson International. He is currently a Non-Executive Director of Yule Catto & Co and is a Fellow of the Chartered Institute of Management Accountants.

Paul Manduca has been an Independent Non-Executive Director of Prudential since 2010 and was appointed Chairman of the Nomination Committee in 2012. Before that Paul was a Non-Executive Director and Senior Independent Director of Wm Morrison Supermarkets plc. (Morrisons). Prior to this Paul was European CEO of Deutsche Asset Management and Global CEO of Rothschild Asset Management as well as founding CEO of Threadneedle Asset Management Limited when he was also a director of Eagle Star and Allied Dunbar.

Harsh Mariwala is the Chairman, Managing Director and founder of Marico. In 1971, he joined the Mariwala family business Bombay

Oil Industries. In 1990, he founded Marico, which is now present in 25 Asian and African markets. Harsh has been presented with the Ernst & Young Entrepreneur of the Year Award (2009) among other management awards.

Luis Maroto was appointed CEO and President of Amadeus in 2011. He was Deputy CEO of Amadeus from 2009 to 2010, with responsibility for overall company strategy as well as line management of the finance, internal audit, legal and human resources functions. In 2003 Luis was appointed CFO. Prior to joining Amadeus in 1999 as Director, Marketing Finance, Luis held several managerial positions at the Bertelsmann Group.

Charlie Mayfield became the John Lewis Partnership's fifth Chairman in 2007. He joined the Partnership in 2000 as Head of Business Development, responsible for business strategy and development for both John Lewis and Waitrose. Charlie joined the Board as Development Director in 2001 and was responsible for developing the Partnership's online strategy. He became Managing Director of John Lewis in 2005 prior to taking up his appointment as Chairman of the Partnership in March 2007. He began his career as an officer in the army and worked for SmithKline Beecham and McKinsey before joining the Partnership. He is also the Government appointed Chair of the UK Commission for Employment and Skills.

Bob McDonald was Chairman of the Board, President and CEO of Procter & Gamble until mid-2013. He also serves on the Board of Directors of Xerox Corporation, among others, and is Chair of the US-China Business Council. He joined Procter & Gamble in 1980. Prior to that he served in the US Army as Captain, Infantry, Airborne Ranger, 82nd Airborne Division.

Graham Mckay was appointed Executive Chairman of SABMiller plc. in 2012. Previously, he was Chief Executive and, prior to that, Group Managing Director. He joined the company in 1978. Graham is also the Senior Independent Non-Executive Director of Reckitt Benckiser Group and a Director of Philip Morris International.

Nancy McKinstry was appointed CEO and Chairman of the Executive Board of Wolters Kluwer in 2003. Prior to that she gained more than a decade of experience at the company. Among other positions, she was CEO of Wolters Kluwer's operations in North America and was a Member of the Executive Board for two years. Previous positions include senior management positions at Wolters Kluwer subsidiaries, the position of CEO of SCP Communications and management positions with Booz & Company.

Carlos Medeiros has been BRMALLS' CEO since the Company was founded in 2006. BRMALLS is the largest shopping mall company in Latin America, with participation in 51 shopping centres, a total gross leasable area of 1.5 million square metres and a market cap of over US$6 billion at the end of 2012. Until 2011, Carlos was a partner of GP Investments, which he joined in 1998. He was also a member of the Board of Directors of leading Brazilian companies including GP Investments, Gafisa, Tele Norte Leste (Oi), Contax, and Internet Group (iG), among others. He began his career as an associate at Salomon Brothers, in New York, where he worked between 1994 and 1998.

Bert Meerstadt was appointed CEO of NS in 2009. Prior to that he served as a CEO for marketing and communication agency Young & Rubicam Europe, Middle East and Africa. He joined Young & Rubicam when Consulting Marketing and Brand Strategies, a company co-founded by Bert in 1992, was acquired by Y&R in

1995. He started his career in 1986 as a consultant with McKinsey & Company.

Luiz de Mendonça has been the CEO of Odebrecht Agroindustrial since 2012. Odebrecht Agroindustrial is one of the largest Brazilian ethanol, sugar and biomass electricity producers, with capacity to process 40 million tonnes of sugar cane, with a corresponding net revenue of US$3 billion. Prior to his current role, Luiz was CEO of Quattor and COO of Braskem's Polyolefins Division. He was also a member of the Board of Directors of leading Brazilian companies including Copesul, Ipiranga Química, Petroquímica, Química, Paulínia, Politeno, CPP and Polialden. Luiz worked at Rhodia for 15 years, where he served as General Manager in Brazil of production, supply, finance and marketing; as an officer in the Latin America chemical division; and as Vice-President of Rhodia USA.

Daljit L. Mirchandani is the former Chairman of Ingersoll-Rand (India) Ltd. and served as its Managing Director until 2008 and President from 1998 to 2008. He served as a Director of Ingersoll-Rand (India) Ltd. until 2010 having joined in 1998. Previously, he held several key positions in the Kirloskar Group, including Executive Director in Kirloskar Oil Engines, Ltd. In 2005, Daljit served as the Chairman of the Karnataka State council of the Confederation of Indian Industries (CII), and in 2007 was nominated by the CII to be the Chairman of the Task Force formed by the Ministry of Agriculture. He served as a Non-Executive and Independent Director of SREI Infrastructure Finance Limited and as a Non-Executive and Independent Director of Praj Industries Ltd. He is also a Member of the Advisory Board of I-Farm Venture Advisors Pvt. Ltd. and a Director of Mahindra Ugine Steel Co. Ltd., Mahindra Forgings Ltd., and Punjab Tractors Ltd.

Geoff Molson is the President, CEO and co-owner of the Club de Hockey Canadien, Inc., Evenko and the Bell Centre. Prior to this he served as Vice-President of Marketing for Molson in Canada, where he played a strategic role in the development of company brands and in strengthening partnerships with key stakeholders. He is a member of the Board of Directors of CHC Group, Molson Coors Brewing Company, Res Publica and member of the Board of Governors of the National Hockey League.

James Muehlbauer was formerly Executive Vice-President, Finance, and CFO for Best Buy Co., Inc., the leading multinational retailer of technology and entertainment products and services. He joined Best Buy in 2002 as Senior Vice-President of enterprise finance. Jim was named Senior Vice-President and CFO of Best Buy's US business in 2006, where he led financial activities supporting Best Buy's retail, merchandising, marketing, supply chain and real estate capabilities.

Dr Gerry Murphy is a Senior Managing Director in the Corporate Private Equity group and Chairman of The Blackstone Group International Partners LLP, the firm's principal European regulated entity. He is based in London and serves as a Director of several Blackstone portfolio companies. Before joining Blackstone in 2008, Gerry spent five years as CEO of Kingfisher plc. He has also served as CEO of Carlton Communications plc., Exel plc. and Greencore Group plc. Earlier in his career he held senior operating and corporate positions with Grand Metropolitan plc. (now Diageo plc.) in Ireland, the UK and the US.

Brian Newman is Senior Vice-President of Strategy and Finance for PepsiCo. A 20-year veteran of PepsiCo, he began his career in the Corporate Strategy Group based in Purchase, then went on to work in three of PepsiCo's four sectors, including PepsiCo Americas Beverage, Europe, Asia, Middle East and Africa. He has spent time in Business Development in Europe and has held Country CFO and Strategy Leadership roles in Canada, Russia and most recently China. Brian was also the Corporate Treasurer for the Pepsi Bottling Group. His current role includes leadership of PepsiCo's Corporate Strategy Team and CFO responsible for PepsiCo's Global Brand Groups across snacks, beverages and nutrition.

Mark Newton-Jones was the CEO of Shop Direct Group from 2003 until 2012. He was originally hired as CEO of Littlewoods which he helped merge with the catalogue retail business of Great Universal Stores. Mark joined Littlewoods from Next.

Marcelo Bahia Odebrecht is CEO of Odebrecht S.A., a holding company present in more than 20 countries across Africa, Asia, Europe and the Americas with reported total revenues of US$41.3 billion in 2012. He is also the Chairman of the Operating Companies of the group. He joined the Odebrecht group in 1992. In 2002, he was appointed CEO of Construtora Norberto Odebrecht, the largest Engineering and Construction Company in Latin America. At the end of 2008, he became CEO of Odebrecht holding company, which is active in several business segments such as engineering and construction, petrochemicals, transportation and logistics, oil and gas, bio-energy, real estate, environmental services, defence and technology and properties. He holds a Bachelor of Civil Engineering from the Federal University of Bahia, Brazil, and an MBA from IMD in Lausanne, Switzerland.

Dr Fritz Oesterle holds a number of positions on supervisory boards of German companies, among them Schwarz Unternehmenstreuhand and Landesbank Baden-Württemberg, and is British Honorary Consul in Stuttgart. He was CEO of Celesio between 1999 and 2011 and member of the Board of Franz Haniel & Cie. GmbH from 2006 until 2009. Previously, he was a founding partner of the law firm Oppenländer, Dolde, Oesterle & Partner.

Sandy Ogg is an Operating Partner in the Private Equity Group, Blackstone. Before joining Blackstone in 2011, he was the Chief Human Resources Officer for Unilever based in London. Prior to Unilever he was Senior Vice-President, Leadership, Learning and Performance at Motorola. Sandy joined Motorola in 1998 in the Change Management/Organization Effectiveness role. Prior to joining Motorola, he spent 15 years as a Leadership Development and Change Management Consultant – clients included Johnson & Johnson, PepsiCo, General Electric and Motorola. He also held positions of President, Center for Leadership Studies; Managing Director, Dove Associates; and Founder, Via Consulting Group. Before consulting, Sandy started as Line Officer for the United States Coast Guard holding various positions doing Search and Rescue activities and becoming a highly decorated Commanding Officer.

Constantino de Oliveira Jr took over as Chairman of Gol's Company's Board of Directors in 2012, having served as Gol's CEO and a member of the Board of Directors from March 2004 to July 2012. He has also served as a member of the Board of Directors of VRG Linhas Aéreas S.A. (the successor of Gol Transportes Aéreos SA) since 2001, having held the position of CEO at the same company from 2001 to 2012. He introduced the 'low-cost, low-fare' concept to the Brazilian civil aviation industry and was elected the Most Valuable Executive in 2001 and 2002 by *Valor Econômico* newspaper. He was also voted a Leading Executive in the logistics sector in 2003 by *Gazeta Mercantil* newspaper, and a Distinguished Executive in the Air Transportation category at the GALA (Galería Aeronáutica Latinoamericana) awards, sponsored by the IATA. From 1994 to 2000, he held the position of Executive Officer at a passenger road transportation company. Constantino earned a degree in Business Administration from the Federal District University, in Brasília, and attended the Executive Program on Corporate Management from the Association of

Overseas Technical Scholarships. He is a member of Gol's People Management and Corporate Governance, Risk, and Financial Policy Committees.

Stephen F. Page was elected Director and Vice-Chairman of United Technologies Corporation in April 2002, and in September 2002 he took on the additional responsibilities of CFO until he retired in April 2004. Steve served as President and CEO of Otis Elevator, an $8bn division of United Technologies from 1997 to 2002. From 1993 to 1997, he was Executive Vice-President and CFO of United Technologies Corporation. Before joining United Technologies, he spent 20 years with Black & Decker, where he served in various legal and financial positions and was Executive Vice-President and CFO from 1990 to 1993. Steve also served on the corporate boards of Lowe's Companies, Paccar and Liberty Mutual, where he was Lead Director and chaired the Risk Committee. He chaired the audit committee for both Lowe's and Paccar. In addition to his corporate duties he served as a trustee at Loyola Marymount University and served as Audit Committee Chairman. He is currently on the Boards of Trustees of Mount Saint Mary's College and The Catholic Education Foundation.

Duncan Painter in October 2011 became CEO of Emap, which changed its market-facing name to Top Right Group in March 2012. His previous roles include Global Product Leader at Experian Marketing Services, Chief Executive Officer of consumer intelligence company ClarityBlue and European Systems Integration Director for Hitachi Data Systems.

Jean-François Palus serves as the Group Managing Director of PPR SA. Jean-François began his career with Arthur Andersen as an Auditor and Financial Advisor after graduating from France's HEC business school in 1984. Before joining the Artemis Group in 2001, Jean-François spent ten years with the PPR Group, where he held several positions, including Deputy CFO for the timber division of Pinault SA, Group Financial Control Director, Store Manager at FNAC, and Corporate Secretary and member of Conforama's Executive Board from 1998 to 2001. Since 2005, Jean-François has been responsible for managing PPR's mergers and acquisitions, reporting to Francois-Henri Pinault, Chairman and CEO of PPR. He has been PPR's CFO and Deputy CEO since 2005 and 2008, respectively. Jean-François joined the PPR Board in 2009 and he is a member of the Supervisory Board of Puma AG and CFAO.

Gregory M. Parker is President of The Parker Companies, which does approximately $400m in annual sales and has about 400 employees. He was the Vice-Chairman of the Research and Development Committee for the National Association of Convenience Stores for four years. Additionally, he served as Chairman of the BP Amoco Marketers Association for three years. He serves on Pepsi's Retail Advisory Council and served on the Coca-Cola Retail Advisory Committee for three years. The Parker Companies was awarded Entrepreneurial Business of the Year by the *Savannah Morning News* for 2012, and was awarded the Retail Innovator of the Year for the Southeast for 2011 by *The Griffin Report*. Greg was the 2005 recipient of the Savannah Urban Entrepreneur Award.

Dalton Philips is Chief Executive of Wm Morrison Supermarkets plc., the UK's fourth largest supermarket group. His retail career began in store management with Jardine Matheson in New Zealand and, later, as Regional Director of the company's Spanish supermarket division. He then spent seven years with Walmart Stores Inc. and was appointed Chief Operating Officer in Germany. In 2005 Dalton left Walmart to work for the Weston family, where he became Chief Executive of Irish department store group Brown Thomas. In 2007 Dalton moved to Canada to become Chief

Operating Officer of another Weston controlled business, Loblaw Companies Limited. Loblaw is Canada's largest food retailer and a leading provider of general merchandise, pharmacy and financial products and services.

Lawrie Philpott is the founder and CEO of Philpott Black. He formerly was the head of Coopers & Lybrand's UK Human Resource Advisory Group. Lawrie has worked with a number of well-known companies from various industries, including British Telecom, Nokia, QinetiQ, Royal Mail and Ulster Bank.

Michael B. Polk has served as President and CEO of Newell Rubbermaid since July 2011, and has been a member of the company's Board of Directors since 2009. Previously, he was President of Global Foods, Home and Personal Care at Unilever, where he was responsible for the development, innovation and marketing of Unilever's $64bn portfolio of categories and brands. He was a member of the Unilever Executive Board from 2007 to 2011. Prior to this, he spent 16 years at Kraft Foods in roles culminating with President of the Asia Pacific Region for Kraft Foods International and President of Nabisco Biscuit & Snacks for Kraft Foods North America. In both positions, he served on Kraft's Management Committee. Before this, Mike spent three years at Procter & Gamble working in manufacturing and research and development in the Paper Products Division. He serves on the Executive Committee of the Board of Directors of the Metro Atlanta Chamber of Commerce. He has a BS in operations research and industrial engineering from Cornell University and an MBA from Harvard Business School.

Andrew Prozes served as CEO of LexisNexis and on the Board of Directors of Reed Elsevier from 2000 until 2010. Today he serves as Chairman of Alert Global Media (ACAMS), Scribestar and Gina's Ink, and serves on the boards of Interactive Data Corporation,

Cott Corporation, Aptidata Corporation and Asset International Inc.

Roberto Prisco Paraiso Ramos has been CEO of Odebrecht Oil & Gas (OOG) since 1997, responsible for engineering and E&P projects in the Northern Sea, Angola and Brazil. OOG provides integrated, customized solutions for the upstream oil industry in Brazil and around the world, with investments of US$3.5bn for the period of 2010 to 2013. Prior to that, Roberto served as executive of Montreal Engenharia, Tenenge, Fillipo Fochi, Monocean, SEBEP and SEAMAL.

Richard Rankin was named CEO of ACH Food Companies, Inc. in October 2008. He directs ACH in refining the strategy of the company by focusing on the grocery sector and identifying opportunities for both organic and growth acquisitions. Prior to becoming CEO of ACH, he was Director of Business Development at ABF, which he joined in 1994 and where he managed strategy and development. He also had responsibility for strategic assessment of all proposed acquisitions. He first joined ABF as Commercial Director for British Sugar UK, then became Managing Director for ABF's ABR division. His next career move was to Business Development Director for ABF's British Sugar Division where he was responsible for the development of new business streams. Prior to joining ABF, Richard was a Regional Sales Manager for Maytag International, and before Maytag, he held roles of increasing responsibility with Unilever plc.

William H. Rogers, Jr. is Chairman and CEO of SunTrust Banks, Inc., the same organization in which he began his career as a member of the Commercial Bank Training Programme in 1980. He is a member of the Board of Directors of the Federal Reserve Bank of Atlanta and the Atlanta Committee for Progress, as well as the National Board of Directors of Operation HOPE. He is also the Chair of the Board of Directors of the Boys & Girls Clubs of Metro Atlanta.

Sir Nigel Rudd was appointed a Non-Executive Director and Deputy Chairman of Invensys in January 2009 and became Chairman in July 2009. He is the Non-Executive Chairman of BAA and of Pendragon. In addition, he is a Non-Executive Director of BAE Systems and Sappi. Sir Nigel was formerly Deputy Chairman of Barclays and Chairman of Alliance Boots and Pilkington.

Parm Sandhu is the Founding Partner of Tamita Consulting (UK) LLP having previously served as CEO of Unitymedia (Germany). Before that Parm spent seven years in senior finance and strategy roles with Telewest Communications (UK) and Liberty Media (US/UK). He serves as a Non-Executive Director and advises financial investors in the TMT sector.

Ron Sandler is Chairman of Ironshore. Previously, he was the Chairman of Northern Rock between 2008 and 2011, appointed by HM Treasury. Prior to that Ron served as Chief Operating Officer of NatWest Group and Chief Executive of Lloyd's of London. His early career was spent with The Boston Consulting Group.

Cláudio Bérgamo dos Santos has been the CEO and Board Member of Hypermarcas, a Brazilian consumer products company with annual revenues of US$ 2 billion, since 2007. As the Investment Officer of Monte Cristalina, he led Hypermarcas' strategy and has actively developed the M&A program that incorporated leading consumer brands since 2001. He started his executive career as Planning Director at Arisco in 1998. Previously, Mr. Santos worked for McKinsey & Co.

Fabio Schvartsman is the CEO of Klabin, a very traditional Brazilian pulp and paper company with net revenues of

US$2.2bn in 2012. He has a graduate and post-graduate degree in Production Engineering from the University of São Paulo and post-graduate degree in Business Administration from Fundação Getulio Vargas. He was the CEO of San Antonio International and CEO of Telemar Participações SA. At Ultrapar (Grupo Ultra), he was CFO (Ultrapar), managing partner (Ultra SA – parent company of Ultrapar), CEO (Ultraprev), Investor Relations Officer, Planning and Control Director and Head of Planning. He also served as Head of the Department of Planning, Head of Development Division and Head of Department of Economic Studies at Duratex. He is a member of the Board of Directors of Duratex, Companhia Brasileira de Distribuição (CBD) and Hospital Israelita Albert Einstein.

Pedro Pereira da Silva is Chief Operating Officer of Portuguese Jeronimo Martins Group and CEO of the company's Polish subsidiary. In the latter role, he led the discount chain Biedronka to its current position as market leader in Poland.

Charles Sinclair became Independent Non-Executive Director of Associated British Foods plc. in 2008 and Chairman in 2009. Prior to that he was Chief Executive of Daily Mail and General Trust plc. for 21 years. He has also been a Senior Independent Director of SVG Capital plc. since 2009 and its Independent Non-Executive Director since 2005. Charles served as a Non-Executive Director of Thomson Reuters plc. and Thomson Reuters Corporation and as a Director of Schroders plc. and Schroder Japan Growth Fund plc. He serves as a Director of Medialaser and as Chairman of the Trustees of the Minack Theatre Trust, Porthcurno, Cornwall.

Benet Slay was appointed CEO of Carlsberg UK in March 2012. Previously, he was Managing Director, Northern Europe between 2009 and 2011 as well as Managing Director GB between 2006 and 2009 for Diageo. Before joining Diageo in 2004, Benet had worked for PepsiCo since 1991 and, prior to that, started as a management accountant at Unilever.

Richard F. Smith is Chairman and CEO of Equifax Inc., which he joined in September 2005 after more than two decades with General Electric Co. Rick's leadership has transformed Equifax, a 114-year-old company, into a leading global information solutions company, with advanced analytics and predictive data. Under his leadership, Equifax employs 7,500 people in 18 countries and has sustained record levels of financial performance and shareholder return. At General Electric Co. he was appointed a Corporate Officer in 1999, and was Chief Operating Officer of General Electric Insurance Solutions before leaving the company. His career at GE also included leadership roles as the President and CEO of the Global Asset Management Division, President and CEO of the Global Leasing Division and numerous leadership positions in the Engineering Thermoplastic Division. A 2010 honoree in the Georgia State University's J. Mack Robinson College 'Business Hall of Fame', Rick was the 2009 Chairman of the Metro Atlanta Chamber of Commerce and now serves on their Board of Directors. He is the 2013 Chairman of the Atlanta Committee for Progress Board and also serves on the board of trustees for The Lovett School.

Tim Steiner is the CEO and one of the founding directors of Ocado. Prior to Ocado, Tim spent eight years as a banker at Goldman Sachs. During his time there he was based in London, Hong Kong and New York in the Fixed Income division.

Sir John Sunderland is a member of the Board Corporate Governance and Nominations Committee, the Board Remuneration Committee and the Board Citizenship Committee of Barclays. He is also Chairman of Merlin Entertainments Limited. Until July 2008 he was Chairman of Cadbury Schweppes plc., having worked at Cadbury's in various roles, including that of Chief Executive, since 1968. Sir John is an Adviser to CVC Capital Partners, an Association Member of Bupa, a Governor of Reading University Council and Chancellor of Aston University. He is also a Non-Executive Director on the Board of AFC Energy plc.

Peter Swinburn is President and CEO of Molson Coors and serves as a member of the Board. He has served in various roles throughout the business and has overseen, at different times, the US, UK and International businesses of Molson Coors. Peter also serves on the Board of Express Inc. and serves in the community as a Member of the Board of Trustees for The Denver Center for the Performing Arts.

Rob Templeman is Deputy Chairman of the British Rail Consortium, the RAC and of Gala Coral. He has more than 25 years' experience in consumer-facing industries, latterly focusing on Private Equity-backed business. He has been the Chief Executive of Harveys Furnishing Group, Homebase and Halfords where he was also the Chairman. Rob recently retired as Chief Executive of Debenhams, a position he has held since 2003 when he led the buyout of the company. He is also Chairman of Graduate Fashion Week and is a Trustee of the charity Children with Cancer.

Paul Todd is Vice-President of Strategy for Marketplaces at eBay Inc. He joined the company in July 2012 and leads the Marketplaces Global Strategy team. Before joining eBay, he was Chief Product Officer at Rearden Commerce, responsible for defining and implementing Rearden's product strategy across all of its existing and emerging service areas. Prior to this, he was a Product Management Director at Google, where he developed product strategy and brought products to market in several key areas, including launching a new hotel product and leading the $700m acquisition of ITA Software. He also led Google Advisor, which uses complex commercial data to create direct user offerings. Prior to Google, Paul was a Partner with McKinsey & Company, where he led the North American high-tech strategy practice. His experience covered online services, consumer and media industries, growth/business strategy, organization development and sales and marketing. Paul holds an MA in Engineering from Cambridge University, where he was awarded a Full Blue in soccer. He is also a Chartered Engineer in the UK.

Douglas D. Tough was appointed Chairman and CEO of International Flavors & Fragrances Inc. in 2010. Previously, he served as the CEO and Managing Director of Ansell Limited and spent 17 years with Cadbury Schweppes plc., where he held a variety of positions including President of Cadbury Beverages International and President of the Africa, India, Middle East and Europe Division. From 2000 to 2003, he was President and CEO of Dr Pepper/Seven Up, Inc. He began his career with Procter & Gamble in 1974 and has been a member of IFF's Board of Directors since October 2008. He joined the Board of Directors of Molson Coors Brewing Company in February 2012.

A. Vellayan is the Executive Chairman of the Murugappa Corporate Board. He is the Chairman of EID Parry (India) Limited and Coromandel International Ltd. He is also on the board of Indian Overseas Bank and Kanoria Chemicals Ltd. He holds a diploma in Industrial Administration from the University of Aston, UK, and a Master's in Business Studies from the University of Warwick Business School, UK.

Sjoerd Vollebregt has been the CEO of Stork, a €2bn industrial company in operation for nearly 200 years, since 2002. Before working for Stork he held positions at Koninklijke van Ommeren, Intexo Holding, Ocean plc. and most recently Exel plc. where he was a member of the Executive Board and Deputy Chief Executive

Freight Forwarding & Technology Divisions Americas–Europe. Vollebregt is a Dutch citizen and studied economics at Erasmus University, Rotterdam. In 1976 and 1980 he participated in the Olympic Games as a sailor, a discipline in which he was World Champion.

Dr Stefan von Holtzbrinck has been CEO of Verlagsgruppe Georg von Holtzbrinck (Trade Publishing, Education and Science, Newspapers and Magazines and Electronic Media and Services) since 2001 and one of the two shareholders in the company. Since joining in 1992, he has held several positions in the company after having worked as an assistant to the board of Kirch-Gruppe from 1990 until 1992. He holds a doctoral degree in Law from LMU Munich.

John Walden joined Argos as Managing Director in 2012, having begun his retail career in the 1990s as Chief Operating Officer of Peapod, a pioneer in online supermarket retailing. He joined Best Buy, the giant US electrical retailer, in 1999 as President of its internet and direct channels division, and over an eight-year career also served as Executive Vice-President, Human Capital and Leadership, and ultimately as Executive Vice-President of its Customer Business Group. John later moved to Sears where, as Chief Customer Officer and Executive Vice-President, he led marketing, merchandising and the internet, catalogue and home services divisions. More recently, he was President and CEO of Inversion Inc., a retail consultancy, and Chief Executive of Activeion Cleaning Solutions.

Mike Walsh is CEO of LexisNexis Legal & Professional, before which he was President and CEO of LexisNexis US Legal Markets. He joined LexisNexis in 2003 as Senior Vice-President, Global Strategy and Business Development, having previously been Director of Strategic Business Development at Home Depot.

Earlier in his career, he was a practising attorney with Weil, Gotshal & Manges LLP in Washington, DC, spent time at General Electric, and served as a strategic management consultant with the Boston Consulting Group. He also co-founded Infirmation.com, an online portal for lawyers, and oversaw the company's merger with Findlaw and then Thomson Reuters.

Paul Walsh was appointed CEO of Diageo in 2000 having made a successful career in Diageo and its predecessor company, Grand Metropolitan and retired from this role in June 2013. He joining GrandMet's brewing division in 1982 and became Finance Director in 1986. He is also a Non-Executive Director of FedEx Corporation, Unilever plc., and Avanti Communications plc. He was previously a Non-Executive Director of Centrica plc. and is a member of the board of trustees of the Prince of Wales International Business Leaders Forum, a member of the Prime Minister's Business Advisory Group, and the lead Non-Executive Director at the UK Department for Energy & Climate Change. Paul is immediate past-Chairman of the Scotch Whisky Association and a former Chairman of the Court of Governors of Henley Management College. Paul has also been appointed Business Ambassador for the food and drink industries by the UK Department for Business, Innovation and Skills.

Chris Weston was appointed President and CEO of Direct Energy in 2009, having previously held numerous leadership roles within Centrica plc., which owns Direct Energy and its operations in North America. Most recently, he was the Managing Director of British Gas Services, a position to which he was appointed in June 2005. He served as Managing Director of British Gas Business between 2002 and 2005, and from 2001 to 2002 was Managing Director of Europe for Onetel, which was acquired by Centrica. Before joining Centrica, he worked for Cable & Wireless in both Australia and the UK.

Michael D. White is Chairman, President and CEO of DIRECTV, where he oversees the strategic direction and operations of one of the world's leading providers of digital television entertainment services. Prior to his appointment he held several senior-level positions in PepsiCo, most recently serving as CEO of PepsiCo International and Vice-Chairman of PepsiCo from 2003 to 2009. Previously he was President and CEO of Frito-Lay's Europe, Africa and Middle East division and CEO of Snack Ventures Europe, PepsiCo's partnership with General Mills International. From 1998 to 2000, he was Vice-President and CFO of PepsiCo. He joined Frito-Lay in 1990 as Vice-President of Planning. Before joining PepsiCo, White was Senior Vice-President and General Manager for Avon Products, Inc. He also worked as a management consultant for Bain & Company and Arthur Andersen & Co. In addition to serving on the DIRECTV Board of Directors, he is a director of Whirlpool Corp.

Iwan Williams joined Premier Foods in 2011 as the Managing Director Grocery and Bakery. His previous roles include President of McCormicks Europe, Middle East and Africa and Strategic Marketing Director of Coca-Cola, Asia Pacific. His earlier career included positions with S.C. Johnson Wax and Cadbury Schweppes.

Zhang Ruimin is the Chief Executive Officer and Founder of the Haier Group. Through 28 years of development, he has turned Haier into the world's largest home appliances brand. Ruimin has integrated the essence of both Chinese and Western management concepts in his pursuit of management innovation. His unique and pioneering thinking and practice have won high recognition from the global management circle. Prof Michael E. Porter, father of competitive strategy, has hailed Ruimin as an 'outstanding strategic thinker'.

Index

Cutting-edge thinking and best learning practice from the world's leading business publisher.

"Does exactly what it says on the tin – and does it brilliantly. This book will become a well-thumbed favorite."

Emma Leech, Director of Marketing - The University of Nottingham

9780273757092

9780273745471

9780273778868

9781292002613

Available to buy online and from all good bookshops (www.pearson-books.com)